Concise History of

HARLEY-DAVIDSON

Concise History of

HARLEY-DAVIDSON

SHAUN BARRINGTON

BARNES &NOBLE BOOKS

This edition published by Barnes & Noble, Inc.
by arrangement with Osprey, a division of Reed Books

© Barnes & Noble Books
© Osprey Publishing

CIP Cataloging Data Available Upon Request.

ISBN 076070 216 0

M 10 9 8 7 6 5 4 3 2 1

Printed in China

Picture Acknowledgements:

Australian War Memorial 63b
Roland Brown 18, 56, 59t, 108, 110b.
Roland Brown/Oli Tennent 68, 112, front of jacket.
Roland Brown/Mac McDiarmid 107t.
Gold & Goose 109t.
Imperial War Museum 62, 63t.
Louise Limb, artist 37, 41, 58, 102, back of jacket.
Andrew Morland 21b, 22t, 25, 36b, 48b, 74b, 109b.
Southampton City Museum 12.
Barrie Smith 3, 7, 9t, 11, 14, 15, 17, 22b, 23, 24t,
31, 35t, 37b, 38t, 40, 42b, c, 44c, 47, 64, 79t, 96, 97, 98, 99,
100, 101, 104, c, 106b, 107b, 110t, 111.
Garry Stuart 9b, 12, 61, 65, 66, 67, 68c, 69, 70, 72tr, b, 73, 81b, 84t.
Mick Walker archive 42t, 44b, 50, 51t, 55, 57, 77, 90b, 103.
Mick Woollett archive 1, 5, 10, 20, 21t,
24b, 26, 27, 28, 29, 30, 34, 37b, 36b, 38b, 39, 40c, 43, 44t, c,
45, 46, 48t, m, 49, 51b, 52, 53, 54, 59b, 71, 74, 75,
76, 78, 79b, 80, 81t, 82, 83, 84b, 85, 86, 87,
88, 89, 90t, 91, 92, 93, 94, 105.

With thanks to Dennis Baldry, and to Mick Walker (chapter 4)
for additional information.

Preparing for war Stateside, August 1940, on Harley-Davidson WLAs.

Contents

TITLE PAGE **FXRT, 1990; not necessarily the most handsome H-D ever produced, but that bulbous-looking fairing gives excellent protection and there's plenty of ground clearance. This machine had been hired from the HOG fly-ride program for a trip through Arizona.**

RIGHT **This 1987 Heritage Softail belongs to photographer Barrie Smith, who supplied many of the photographs in this book. He regularly tours in Europe – the picture was taken in South West France at Castera Verduzan. 1987 was the first year of the Custom model, with passing lights, leather bags and screen as standard. Barrie's machine is fitted with Mikuni HS40 carb, high lift cam, and a derestricted exhaust.**

Introduction

The Hog With Nine Lives

Everybody knows what a Harley-Davidson is. Not an earthshattering observation you might say. Most people know what a Suzuki is, even a Triumph Bonneville. They're motorcycles, right? The difference is that everybody knows what a Harley-Davidson *sounds* like, what it *looks* like, even what it represents, when it comes to aspirations, dreams, image. The universal high profile of Harley-Davidson today is an important key to understanding the long history of the company: and part of the fascination with that history is that it really shouldn't have been that long. It might seem a strange way to begin a history of these marvelous machines to look at what could have stopped the company dead in its tracks on several occasions, for different reasons, through its 90-year history. But a brief look at how Harley-Davidson overcame the bad times is a good way to highlight just what made it so strong; and it is also a way of debunking some of the myths. Harley-Davidson has earned a reputation in some quarters as a dinosaur, decades behind the British in the 1950s, eons behind the Japanese from the 1960s to the present day. If this were the whole story, how could H-D wrest back from the Honda Gold Wing its position as the leading big bike seller in the US? There certainly were some technological innovations, and some of them were vital to the company, from Bill Harley's springer forks to the 1984 Evo V2 engine. But they were changes of a particular kind, almost unique to the H-D philosophy, the H-D way of going about things. They are not in the same category as, say, the double conrods on the

oval pistons and single-sided swingarm of the 1992 Honda NR750. What use would Harley-Davidson have made of the famous Moto Guzzi wind tunnel back in the 1950s, partly responsible for that company's revolutionary unit construction of engine and transmission? No, H-D innovations have almost always been based upon a careful refinement of that which has gone before, and a belief that power and strength – to include the *appearance* of strength – are what the Harley-Davidson rider wants, not cutting edge technical ingenuity. Power, in this case, does not mean speed: it means torque. And strength means steel, not composite materials. Harley-Davidson would never hide the engine beneath carbon fiber, it must be seen for what it is, a big, slow turning V-twin with its own very special voice.

The first problem the company faced in 1903 was faced by all of the many hundreds of tiny concerns, both in Europe and the US, who thought that there just may be a market for the motor bicycle, invented (or rather, first designed) by Gottlieb Daimler 18 years earlier. That problem simply evaporated for Harley-Davidson because of the people involved. Deciding to build motorcycles for a living was not really a sensible career move back then. Not only was there no indication whether anyone would possibly buy such a noisy, dangerous machine, nobody even knew the best place to put the engine in the frame. Harley-Davidson, however, had just the right personnel to sort out the problems: a machinist, a draftsman, a patternmaker and a toolmaker. Not only were these men technically

LEFT **61 cu in V-twin, from around 1915. The "V" configuration was first settled on by Bill Harley in 1909. The 45-degree angle has no particular advantage – in fact it is at a distinct disadvantage in comparison with the 75 degrees of the Yamahas (their first vee being the 981cc 1981 TRI tourer) or the super smooth 90-degree Ducatis. But would it even enter the heads of H-D designers to change it and endanger that unique sound and look? They are not that foolish.**

sound, they were financially cautious, loyal to each other (as friends and relations) and had a real passion for technical advances. Where so many fell at the first hurdle – the challenge of transforming a hobby and a hunch into a manufacturing company, these men had all the right qualities to make the breakthrough, particularly as their personal skills and temperaments complemented one another.

Their caution however, more than their innovative abilities, is what marks the first successful machine produced by the three Davidson brothers, Walter, Arthur and William, and family friend Bill Harley. The "Silent Gray Fellow", produced in 1905, was revolutionary not in its design, but in its durability. Its wheels were unusually strong and heavy (there, from the very beginning, the emphasis on strength), its engine was upgraded from the French original, the front forks were heavy gauge. The company's founders had realised almost immediately, at the very beginnings of the motorcycle industry, that speed, performance, were luxuries which could be worked for once the machine in question didn't blow up or fall apart. A lot of other designers, in the US and across the world, never

learned that first simple lesson, and disappeared like tire smoke…

And how many motorcycles had Herr Daimler produced over the last twenty years? Well actually just the one, with its wooden frame and stabilisers. He of course had moved on to a far more practical application of the internal combustion engine:

BELOW **Harley-Davidson have sometimes eaten the dust in their long and fascinating history, but never for very long. Leo Anthony Jnr in trouble on a Forty Five (probably a WR) at Daytona in 1993. No lasting damage to machine or rider.**

survived that particular crisis, as it does the company's strategy following the world economic meltdown of October 29, 1929. "We may be able to keep you on until the spring" was the baleful comment of William A. Davidson, as 5000 banks failed and Excelsior, the third big motorcycle manufacturer, faded away.

Of course not all crises to beset Harley-Davidson through its long history were as momentous, nor were they all "situations beyond our control." Even the most obsessed H-D fan or company

Until the AMF era, Harley-Davidson never got over-excited when it came to buying in new plant machinery. They never tooled up too quickly, before the technology was proven. But they were proud of this machine, photographed in 1958, drilling 74 cu in cylinder heads in one operation with multi drill inserts.

which points to another key moment when one of the Hog's nine lives was threatened. By the beginning of the 1920s, not only had Henry Ford revolutionised industrial production methods and transportation for ever: he was even dumping hundreds of thousands of cars at below cost (and so was GM). The Model T cost just $400, the two seater £265. Harley-Davidson production in 1921 was a third of what it was the previous year, while the capacity was undiminished, in fact had expanded. How could *any* motorcycle manufacturer survive this auto revolution? Bear in mind that the company at this time was still playing second fiddle to Indian, their Scout hounding the 1919 H-D Sport Twin to oblivion by 1922.

Chapter Two explains how Harley-Davidson

marketing guru would not claim that every Milwaukee product has emerged from the well springs of engineering genius fully formed. The side valve 74 cu in VL of 1929, for example, was so underpowered that the engine had to be completely overhauled. The machine was extremely heavy, and the flywheels were very small, in an attempt to improve acceleration,which meant – the ultimate horror for a Harley – lack of torque. It is worth dwelling upon this problematic design a little, because it reveals in microcosm many of the end-lessly repeated patterns discernible in Harley-Davidson history, the attitudes and reactions to problems which have now made the company one of the most famous in the world. The VL V-twin was supposed to replace the long-running J series of machines which had been gradually improved. Note *improved*, not radically overhauled at any one moment. The sturdy J-11 had been introduced way back in 1915, and its inlet over exhaust layout had survived right up until the first year of the 74 cu in VL. As an example, in 1925 Bill Harley had con-

Ron Stratman's Buffalo Glide at the Sturgis Rally. Why follow the Herd? Harley-Davidson, uniquely, invites freedom of expression.

Excelsior, both bad for business, and bad for PR.

So what happened? The company replaced the small flywheels, which meant a larger crankcase; they redesigned the cams and finally gave the VL a new frame. While this very expensive overhaul was going on, Walter Davidson was keeping the dealers in line, assuring them that everything would come good, and the company was quietly ensuring its dominance of the AMA (American Motorcycle Association) the organization which represented motorcycle interests, while Indian was looking the

tracted Arthur Constantine Jnr to "redesign" the 74 cu in J. What he did was lower the frame and replace the tank, an update which cost practically nothing but kept the machine looking fresh. Even a front brake wasn't considered necessary on the 61 cu in V-twin until 1927.

Somehow you just can't see Mr Soichiro Honda nodding sagely in agreement with the dictum: "If it ain't broke, don't fix it." But it's as if it was written for Bill Harley. So if the company were so careful with the introduction of new technology, what went wrong with the VL? For one thing, they were looking at the opposition, not just at their own need to update. Indian had been having considerable success with the side-valve configuration for some time. When rumors of the VL's shortcomings began to spread, some law enforcement agencies canceled orders and some dealers defected to Indian or other way, distracted from its core business. At the same time, H-D had released the model C, a 30.5 cu in side-valve single cylinder which overheated and didn't have the V-twin Harley stamp of authority. It used the same frame as the larger models, with consequent lack of performance. It would disappear (in the US) in 1934. In addition, in 1929, the Flathead 45 was introduced.

So why does this muddle at the end of the 1920s act as a kind of paradigm of what is good, tough, about Harley-Davidson right to the present day?

First of all, the company had the dealer network, the (relatively) solid market position to survive the VL error, and the sheer common sense to sort the whole thing out by the following year. Secondly, the C model was more or less abandoned to wither on the vine, while the 45 Flathead V-twin would survive until 1973 – think about it, 1973 – and prove to be Harley's longest lived powerplant. And side-valve was seen at the time as a step *backwards* by some: but the new Flathead could compete with ohv and even F head (intake over exhaust) configura-

LEFT **American troops and MPs embark for France in August 1944, riding standard 1942 WLAs. This is Southampton on the south coast of England. The H-D contribution in both World Wars is extremely impressive – and they managed to do it without jeopardising their own viability, unlike Indian in the First World War.**

tions, at the same time as being easier to service. While H-D was being hit as hard as everyone else by the stock market crash therefore, it still had the muscle to redesign what could have been a disaster (the VL), write off at least for the home market a single cylinder machine (the 30.5 cu in "baby Harley") and using no fundamentally new technol-

ogy, produce an incredibly successful dynasty of smaller machines. Why is this short period so typical of the company, echoing other changes, other problems, other eras?

Well, being distracted by what the opposition are doing would happen again; H-D would produce a scooter just as the market began to decline in the

BELOW **Sportster with real snakeskin trim at the Rat's Hole Custom Show at Sturgis. Held on the Thursday of Sturgis Week, it's the Holy Day for bike art.**

early 1960s for example, tempted by the success of all those little Italian imports – and that's a very minor example of chasing a market that was never going to be part of the H-D sphere of influence, there are in fact more serious ventures in to unknown territory. Secondly, the strength to turn around the VL teething problems quickly and with-

out alienating the core buyers of the big V-twins is fundamental. Of the nineteen models on offer for 1997, love them or hate them, nothing will drop off, as it had done on occasion in the 1960s in particular, under Aermacchi/Italian influence; but even then, the H-D mystique prevailed, through some shrewd damage limitation. Thirdly, while everyone else was, hardly surprisingly, in turmoil following the Wall Street Crash, Harley-Davidson was getting closer to its buyers and closing the door on its rivals by coming to dominate the AMA. The marketeers at H-D today are clearly superb, and they were then. "Any Harley-Davidson you want! Our savings club plan … $2.50 starts you!"

The "Baby" Harley is significant on two counts. One, H-D has never produced a smaller motorcycle which has seriously troubled its foreign competitors, despite having produced (and sold) many; and two, it may have been unavailable in the US after 1934, but you could still buy one in Japan in 1937. Exports have often been vital at different times in H-D history. In 1994, about 30% of the company's output was exported – and that was very much in a

RIGHT **The 1997 FLSTS Heritage Springer, exposed spring front end for that authentic forties/fifties look. Tooled and fringed leather comes as standard. V2 Evolution engine of course, like all of today's Harleys. The H-D catalog informs the prospective buyer: "We call this one The Ol' Boy." For many, a dream machine, worthy of a little soft focus!**

domestic seller's market, with some US dealers apparently begrudging the loss. It seems to the author that H-D were merely being sensible, remembering the past and not dismissing export earnings, at the same time maintaining their hard-won worldwide presence and keeping the home market hungry. The Forty Five Flathead symbolises sound engineering, robust design, and longevity, all the best H-D traits.

So here's the H-D recipe for success:

1 Keep your eye on the ball. Don't worry too much about the opposition.

2 Maintain a vigorous marketing strategy and get as close to the customer as you can; events like Sturgis have now become "unofficial" H-D events.

3 Export.

4 Develop technology at the right pace: evolution, not revolution.

All of the above, of course, doesn't amount to a hill of Honda SJ50s, if you don't have something to sell, something people want. It is fair to say that from 1907, H-D have always had that, in some form or other. And most of the time, the basis, the first building block of that form, has been the big V-twin engine.

This brings us to another of the Hog's nine lives. In 1948, Mr Soichiro Honda, the son of a black-smith, began making motorcycles. In 1954, he visited the Isle of Man to size up the opposition, and in 1961, Hondas won the 125 and 250cc T.T. races. Three years earlier, the C100 Super Cub was born, the most successful personal transport in history: in terms of numbers, it makes VW Beetles look like exotica. In 1966, the 305cc Honda CB77 Super Hawk was producing maximum power at 9000 revs, incredible for a road bike. The 1968 CB750 offered four-cylinder motorcycling, disc brakes, five speeds, 124mph, great styling and electric start, all at a bargain price. Today, the RFV750R RC45 is a 16-valve V4 capable of 175mph with race kit. Honda is the most successful motorcycle manufacturer ever. There may be one or two other Japanese manufacturers you could name – maybe three – but

the main reason for some edited highlights of Honda is the existence of another star in its hugely varied and technically formidable firmament. The golden wing was recognised all over the world when the company christened their new 1000cc four-cylinder model in 1975. After that, the Honda Gold Wing just growed and growed: by 1988 it had an extra two cylinders and 1520cc. Even more alarming, in 1981, production had moved from Japan to Ohio. There are more than 65,000 members of Gold Wing owner's clubs worldwide, and that 1988 machine was the biggest bike ever built in the US.

The biggest? The most complex? In the home of the big Harley? Yup, *and* it outsold the home grown leviathan for a while. (But note: only for a while.)

To take firstly the invasion of smaller motorcycles from Honda, then Suzuki and Yamaha, lastly Kawasaki, which started in earnest in the late 1950s with two stroke machines which attracted the motorcycle newcomer. This was not something which could be ignored by H-D, because those newcomers would soon trade up to larger displacement models. The company updated its own smaller machines, such as the 125cc "Hummer," which became the 165cc "Super Ten" in 1960. Following the industry trend of using plastics instead of metal for some components, H-D bought 60% of the stock of the Tomahawk Boat Company, who had the necessary technical knowledge on tap and could

RIGHT 1995 FLHTCI Ultra Classic Electra Glide. Top of the range, top of the world.

help in the production of windshields, saddle bags, Servi-Car bodies etc. Electric start was finally offered in 1965 on the FL and FLH Duo Glide models for the first time, as it had been on most of the Japanese models for years. In this way, H-D kept up with developments as far as possible, but its percentage of the overall US motorcycle market was slipping. For the first time in its history, the company issued shares in the same year to raise capital.

But what really kept H-D from losing even more of the market at this time was not just these sterling efforts. It was loyalty, and it was the unique nature of the big Harley-Davidson V-twin. The core of H-D enthusiasts continued to trade in their motorcycles for more of the same every year or so.

There was just nothing like it, and there still isn't. And ten years later, that includes the Gold Wing. Big, yes: (1991 GL1500/6 was 811 lb). A luxurious, technically exotic – water cooled – tourer you just can't ignore, with linked brakes, twin discs at the front, one at the back.

It has a digital clock, loud speakers, adjustable windscreen and air pressure control for the rear suspension.

But it's not a Glide. It's a flat six, so of course it doesn't sound like a Harley-Davidson. You can't see that engine at all; the discs have plastic covers. One UK journalist commented in 1993 that with the latest Gold Wing, the designers had "obviously been keeping an eye on recent developments in bathroom fittings." Well over half a million Gold Wings have been sold, but not even this direct challenge in the large capacity bike arena could shake the faith of the H-D aficionado, or dent the marque's unique symbolic position as "The great American Freedom Machine." An H-D advertisement from the early 1980s reveals just how well the company knew what it had:

"Motorcycles by the people for the people. A Harley-Davidson is not overweight; don't compare a Harley with some little lightweight bike; there is a world of difference and we'd like to keep it that way ... Simplicity of design is the best way to insure durability ... We only use one carburetor. You don't pay for four and the hassles later ... We don't turn out motorcycles like popcorn ... There's a lot of careful hand work ... There's no better place to put your money."

This is adman-speak admittedly, but it's pretty much the truth. And don't you love that sniffy reference to "some little lightweight bike!"

The level of awareness of Milwaukee's finest across the world, and the intense desirability of the H-D V-twin will always be something of a mystery; and only a few of the potential threats to the company's very survival, to the Hog's nine lives, have been touched on in this introduction. It is almost impossible to think of an equivalent story in any industry, let alone in transportation. The closest the author can think of is the massive, instant success of the Ford Mustang in 1964. That car was somehow more than the sum of its parts. The closest parallel is that it was available to everyone – just as H-D riders are accountants, pop stars and outlaws – and that each car could be 'customised' with a massive list of options. A million were sold in quick time: but everyone was different. Somehow, this feels like the USA at its very best, democracy in action. The same goes for the success of Harley-Davidson, born in a backyard shed ninety years ago.

Founding Fathers

A Quick Getaway

"When something works, we stick with it."
(H-D brochure, 1989)

No time to waste. There's a lot to get through, and only a limited number of pages: it certainly didn't take Harley-Davidson long to produce motorcycles in impressive numbers. It didn't take long for a machinist to become a company president, a student/draftsman a chief engineer; a patternmaker was quickly a secretary/general sales manager and a railroad toolmaker became a works manager.

At the beginning of the century, everyone was taking up the challenge of motorcycle production at breakneck speed; by 1902 the Hendee Manufacturing Company was already building the Indian out on the east coast. The drill was: get a bicycle frame and attach an engine to it - wherever took your fancy - and sell it. This is more or less what William Harley and Arthur and Walter Davidson did in 1903, (without the sale). They put a single-cylinder engine based upon the DeDion design into a tube bicycle frame and painted the frame in gloss black. It is unlikely that these three were determined to go into production, but admiring words from friends and family and some vague inquiries as to price saw two more produced the following year, eight sales in 1905, and then bam! Fifty machines in 1906. By 1909 there were 35 employees, and by 1920 there were 2000 dealerships worldwide.

How did they succeed where so many others failed? As suggested in the introduction, they were the right men for the job, at the right time. The machinist and first company president was Walter Davidson Snr. He worked for the Chicago, Milwaukee and St Paul Railroad, and would join

RIGHT **Walter Davidson, first president of the Harley-Davidson Motor Company, pictured after victory in the Long Island Endurance Race of 1908.**

LEFT **you don't just have to sell motorcycles to individuals; stress the economic running costs and there is a huge potential utility machine market, which H-D went for from the very beginning. Delivering the mail on a 35 cu in single cylinder H-D, in 1911.**

the adventure only when his brother Arthur's hobby, (for that's what it was, literally tinkering about in the backyard) turned into a genuine moneymaking concern.

William S. Harley - Bill - was a bicycle fitter at 15; he had the brains to become an apprentice draftsman, then later showed the ability to use those brains ,when he realised he needed more of a grounding in engineering if he were to contribute more to the project, and went off to study at the University of Wisconsin. He would be designing H-Ds right up to the outbreak of the Second World War.

The patternmaker was Arthur Davidson, whose contribution would be in that area in which, perhaps, his brothers and his friend Bill Harley might have failed, even they had been the greatest engineers with the greatest motorcycles of the age. He knew how to sell: or at least, he learned how to do it very quickly. By 1910, he was busily setting up a dealership network across the country.

In between "design" and "sell" there is "produce." Enter eldest brother William, the railroad toolmaker and foreman. As Works Manager, he would be responsible for buying production

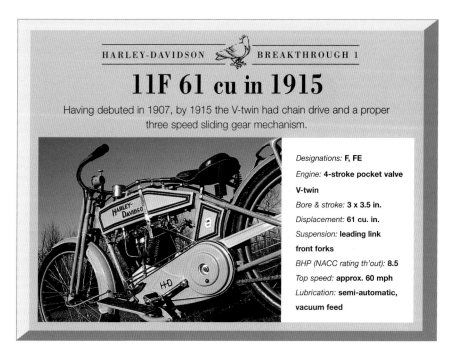

HARLEY-DAVIDSON   BREAKTHROUGH 1

11F 61 cu in 1915

Having debuted in 1907, by 1915 the V-twin had chain drive and a proper three speed sliding gear mechanism.

Designations: **F, FE**

Engine: **4-stroke pocket valve V-twin**

Bore & stroke: **3 x 3.5 in.**

Displacement: **61 cu. in.**

Suspension: **leading link front forks**

BHP (NACC rating th'out): **8.5**

Top speed: **approx. 60 mph**

Lubrication: **semi-automatic, vacuum feed**

Model 23J 61 cu in 1923

The same, but so much better; it's a "breakthrough" in itself to stick with what works. Better cam/valve action and better lubrication.

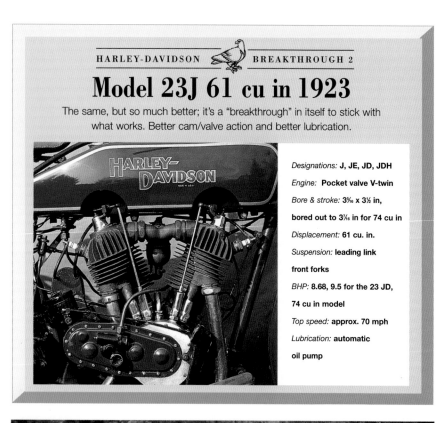

Designations: **J, JE, JD, JDH**

Engine: **Pocket valve V-twin**

Bore & stroke: **3⁵⁄₁₆ x 3½ in,**
bored out to 3⁷⁄₁₆ in for 74 cu in

Displacement: **61 cu. in.**

Suspension: **leading link**
front forks

BHP: **8.68, 9.5 for the 23 JD,**
74 cu in model

Top speed: **approx. 70 mph**

Lubrication: **automatic**
oil pump

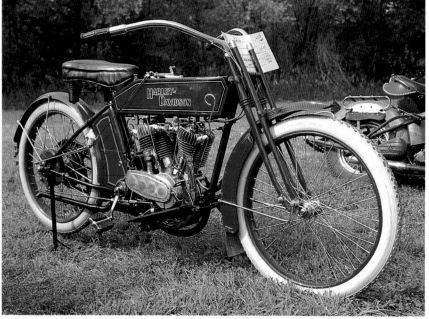

ABOVE **Between the engine pictured at the top and the one above there are a decade's worth of refinements, such as round-edged cooling fins; but they are both V-twins.**

machinery and overseeing the workforce as it grew (at an extraordinary rate) , right up until his death in 1937.

It was a dream team and there were other factors which helped. First of all, it was a family affair, which helped to bind the company together; and Arthur and Bill Harley had been schoolfriends and had worked together in Milwaukee's Barth Manufacturing Company. Their family ties would stand the company in good stead in years to come, as a second and third generation (the most famous being grandson Willie G) entered the business. In the mid-1960s, when the company sold shares for the first time, a controling majority of voting shares were held by more than 50 members of the Harley and Davidson families!

Secondly, the founders were genuine motorcycling enthusiasts. In 1908, Walter won the New York Endurance Run on a standard belt-driven H-D single, from Catskill to Brooklyn and around Long Island. He then immediately followed this up with victory in the FAM Economy Run on the Island, garnering excellent publicity for Arthur in his drive to establish franchises. (it was only William who didn't ride).

LEFT AND BELOW
A rather unusual sight to say the least! That's a 1913 racer being given a tow by a 1917 roadster, at Sturgis in 1990. The brakeless racers could reach terrifying speeds on the board tracks.

THREE-TIMES LUCKY

If anyone deserved a little luck it was these men, poised to give the world something to enjoy for a century, and they got it. A short cut to understanding the workings of the DeDion engine was provided by the input of Emil Kruger, a German immigrant working at the Barth Manufacturing Company with Arthur and Bill; and marine engine designer Ole Evinrude just happened to live around the corner from the Davidson household - he knew a lot about carburetors.

All of the early machines were hand built in a tiny shed (10 x 15 ft) put up by William in the family backyard, housing a drill press and a lathe. It would have been impossible to build 50 machines in

RIGHT AND BELOW
Hardly surprisingly, the early Harley-Davidsons are collector's pieces today. The early twin (right) is in the window of the venerable Dudley Perkins dealership in San Francisco apart from selling H-Ds practically from the word go, another claim to fame is the introduction by Perkins of race engineering genius Tom Sifton to the marque (See chapter four). Similarly, the machine below caused a great deal of interest when photographed in 1982 at the Pioneer Run, when nearly 70 years of age.

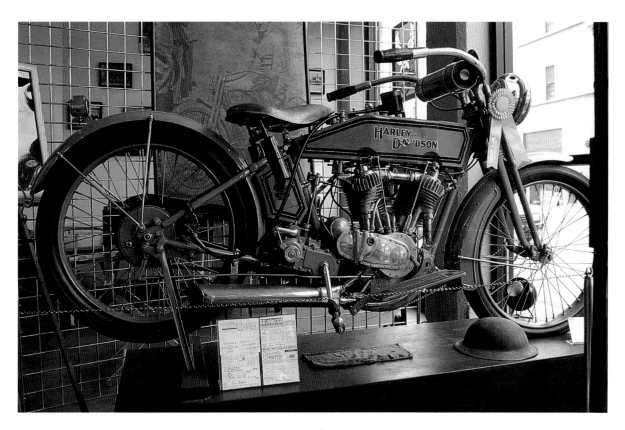

such a place, and lucky stroke number three was the willingness of wealthy maternal uncle James McLay to loan the money for a land purchase at Juneau Avenue, the famous traditional home of H-D. There was nothing radical about those early single cyclinder machines, except that they didn't break as often as some of the offerings from other backyard sheds across the country! Having upped the performance of the standard DeDion engine with a 3-in bore and

3.5-in stroke and heavier castings on the prototype, Bill Harley and Arthur realised that the frame had to be stonger than just that of a pedal bicycle, so made one, from heavy gauge tubing and extra thick forks. The loop frame was much stronger than the "traditional" if that's the right word for the product of a fledgling industry, diamond shape.

SPRINGER FORKS

What was new, was Bill Harley's answer to a pressing difficulty faced by all motorcycle manufacturers at the time. How to soften the ride, particularly at the front. Two unsprung legs were attached to two sprung legs just in front via a pair of forged steel links at the bottom. Bill Harley thought up this ingenious solution in his final year of study at the University of Wisconsin.

It allowed for low stress levels on the forks, but with adequate wheel travel. The H-D sprung front fork would feature for many years. It was relatively simple, it was strong, it was easy to maintain - it's got "Harley-Davidson" written all over it! But it would cause handling problems when speeds

increased. Aware that engine noise was a genuine problem, if the motorcycle was ever to be accepted as a form of mass transport rather than an amusement, H-D produced excellent silencers from the very beginning; so much so that the single-cylinder machine produced between 1904 and 1908 was known as the "Silent Gray Fellow."

In 1909 the 5-35 model offered 35 cu in and 5 bhp, a significant improvement. In the same year, Bill Harley tried something which would change the history of motorcycling for ever. He took two standard 5-35 cylinders on a common crankshaft and arranged them at a 45-degree angle. Nobody got carried away: just a few V-twins were built in 1909, and none in 1910, waiting for the new "pocket valve" (inlet-over-exhaust) to replace the old De Dion type atmospheric inlet.

The V-twin design meant built-in vibration at higher engine speeds, (anything over 4000 revs) and there were limits imposed on cylinder bore size by the narrow angle between cylinders, so a slow turning, long stroke, high torque machines was more or less inevitable. The model 5 D twin was added to the range in 1909. Its actual capacity was 61 cu in

and the engine incorporated a Schebler carburettor. Other mechanical improvements and new developments followed.

In 1912 Harley-Davidson introduced the first really effective motorcycle clutch incorporated in the rear hub with a free wheel unit and offered all chain drive as an option to replace the traditional belts. Belts had advantages over chains in the early days, being not only cheaper but more forgiving to the frame as they stretched with the torque from the engine. Early chains from Indian and others had tended to break. For the 1912 H-D machines, frame distortion was not so much of a problem. Also new was the "Ful-Floteing" saddle, mounted on a sprung seat pillar. This must have been a boon on the unmetalled and potholed country roads of the period.

In 1913 the famous "Step Starter" enabled the rider to start his engine by pushing on either footboard while still seated on the machine. The two-speed gearbox, internal expanding brake, and the carburettor choke were all introduced in that year. The three-speed gearbox and clutch assembly appeared in 1915. Unlike the two-speeder, which

ABOVE **The 30.5 cu in Model C "Baby Harley" of 1929; a reminder that single cylinder machines would not disappear in favor of the big V-twins for many years.**

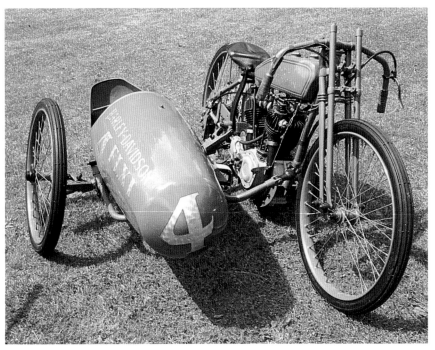

ABOVE **September 1916, this is the first class of pupils at the Harley-Davidson School of Instruction for Army Officers. It soon became clear that without maintenence knowledge within the Army, the motorcycles ordered would quickly become redundant. All three of the big motorcycle manufacturers had service schools established after the war, to train dealers.**

was rear hub mounted, the new, heavier box was an enclosed sliding gear type with a multi plate clutch mounted on the countershaft. Because of its extra weight, it was positioned more logically for balance directly behind the engine.

The period between 1912 and 1920 was a golden one for the motorcycle. Harley-Davidson themselves succeeded in becoming the largest single manufacturer, partly as a result of the military sales boost brought about by the United States' participation in the Great War.

However, all the major manufacturers did well and it should not be forgotten that Harley-Davidson very definitely took third place behind

LEFT **A 1921 989 cc track racer.** It was on a similar capacity machine that D H Davidson (no relation) had first broken 100 mph at Brooklands. H-D's famous "Wrecking Crew" were dominant in competition when the company decided to pull out in 1922. Whether racing one of the early motorcycles, or sitting in the sidecar and entrusting it to someone else (top left, opposite) is worse, is difficult to decide.

Indian and Excelsior for much of this pioneering period.

For the Harley-Davidson company, sales were simply outstanding from 1912 to 1920. This was the period during which motorcycles, both in solo and sidecar form, were a much cheaper form of transport than the car. Henry Ford's Model T of 1909 cost three times as much as a comparable motorcycle and sidecar. It really looked as if that early hunch that the motorcycle was more than just an amusement, that it could be a genuine option for mass personal transportation, had been solid gold. Thirty-four successful manufacturers provided a great choice of machines, which came to include the remarkable Henderson and Pierce four-cylinder models. The utility market was one which Walter would pursue throughout this period with his usual acumen and vigor. As early as 1909 Walter Davidson sold machines to the rural mail delivery agency. The Bell Telephone Company, other various public utilities and police forces also began to buy Harley-Davidson machines.

THE FIRST WORKS RACERS

This was also a period in the history of American motorcycling when racing was very popular and made a very significant contribution to the success of Harley-Davidson, with or without the active support of the company. The old adage "racing improves the breed," if followed too closely, can turn out to be a gloriously uncommercial proposition – say, Aston Martin or Velocette – or exactly right, for a long time – say, Norton. The H-D approach was cautious, but effective.

Two privately entered H-Ds in the 1913 San Diego-Phoenix Desert Race had been beaten out of sight, and it just may have been this humiliation which hastened the development of a decent three-speed gearbox for the V-twin. Note that they were

private entrants: that way, the company can bask in reflected glory if anyone succeeds, but can wash its hands of the failure of "non-Works" machines. It's a strategy used by many manufacturers through the years. Finally, in 1914, H-D could not ignore the publicity gains of competition and Bill Harley took on William Ottaway to oversee works racing. After a few quiet runouts, the company took the Venice,

California road race and won in Dodge City, both in 1915, Otto Walker riding. The midwest racer was up against works teams from Indian, Excelsior, Pope and others on both occasions.

It is somehow fitting that in the Dodge road race a Cyclone motorcycle of an extremely advanced design tore off at the start and nearly lapped the field after three laps. 100 miles in, the chain

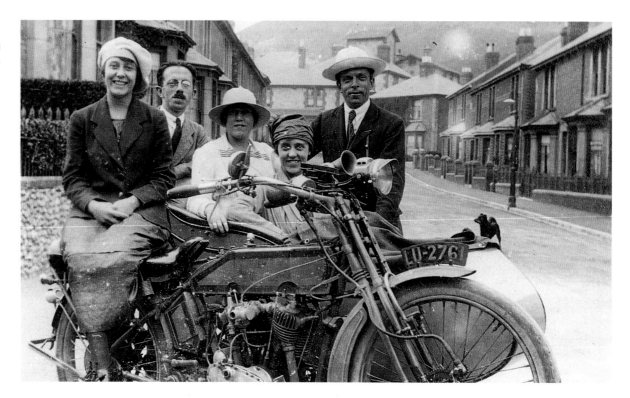

snapped; similarly, Indian and Excelsior fell by the
wayside on the 90th lap. All six of the H-Ds would
finish: slowly, slowly, catchee monkey … Bill
Ottaway produced an eight valve engine with special camshafts and modified ports for the II-K
model which Ottaway rode to win on the board
ovals. The publicity really did work, and production targets were upped to 15,000 units for 1916.

15,000? Apologies for the sudden leaps in numbers which characterise the early history of H-D.
Admittedly, a few pages back we were in a shed
with a second hand lathe! But that really was how
it happened.

By 1915, there were 1500 employees, and by
1918, with war production a vital factor, Harley-
Davidson was the largest motorcycle manufacturer
in the world. The motorcycles were continually
refined throughout this magical era, with a Bosch
electrical system introduced in 1915, replaced after
the war for fairly obvious reasons by components
from Remy, which were in turn considered too
unreliable and eventually replaced by H-D's own
system.

Which is a reminder of another aspect of production, not only in this period but right up to the
present day. H-D was always keen to service the

aftermarket itself. For example, the Rogers Company supplied sidecars for Harley-Davidson up until 1925, but from then on H-D produced them for themselves.

(The names of the Rogers sidecar units have always seemed highly appropriate as H-D fortunes began to tumble from their postwar dizzy heights into the 1920s slump. 1920-21 sidecars were called "Jenny," "Joy" and "Meadow." 1922-23 saw "Plot," "Purity" and "Puritan." 1924-25 produced the "Rescue" and the "Slash!")

EXPORT OR DIE

One of the key elements of Harley-Davidson did not come into play until 1914. By then, main rivals Indian and Excelsior were exporting worldwide.

Having consolidated the home market, with dealerships across the country, H-D appointed Scotsman Duncan Watson as a UK distributor.

He received the first 350 machines in April that year, and would be a prime contact in the establishment of dealerships in Paris, Brussels, Amsterdam and Copenhagen. In Great Britain, the motorcycles found a primed market, familiar with Indian imports since 1908; and guess what? The vast majority of machines sold were V-twins. The singles hardly figured. Perhaps even more than at home, the twin was king.

In 1913 Indian produced more than 31,000 of the 71,000 motorcycles made in the US, the leading manufacturers by a long way. One of the reasons that they did not emerge from the war years with that domination intact was the decision to build

LEFT **H-D's F-head V-twins had been improved in 1917 with the addition of the eight-valve racing machine's four-lobe cams. By 1920, only the Sixty-One and the Sport flat twin were in production.**

The Rodney C Gott
Motorcycle Museum,
named after AMF's
Chairman, opened in
1977 in York,
Pennsylvania. Early
competition and road
models are of course a
major crowdpuller.

20,000 machines (more or less their entire annual output) for the war effort on a perilously tight margin, which would be eroded by inflation. They asked just $187.50 for a solo, plus $49.50 for a sidecar. In contrast, H-D promised 7,000 machines and kept their eyes firmly on domestic sales, (reserving about 10,000 bikes for it), forever strengthening and expanding the dealer network. Those seven thousand machines (plus enough spares for many thousand more) were enough for H-D to trumpet their contribution – as did all of the motorcycle manufacturers, from Rudge-Whitworth in England, to Terrot in France – to the conflict, but it was not a commitment which would endanger domestic income. In fact, it could only be a good thing, allowing expansion of production without risk.

WARTIME EXPANSION

By the time peace was declared in 1918, the US motorcycle industry had received contracts to supply 2600 Excelsior, 1500 Cleveland, 26,500 Harley-Davidson, and a massive 40,000 Indian machines. With the exception of the Cleveland lightweight 221 cc two-stroke, most came with a sidecar. By the end of 1918, about 14,500 H-Ds and 18,000 Indians had actually been delivered and all other contracts were cancelled.

Many machines were sold off in Europe as war surplus which opened up the market by making people aware of the joys of the big V-twin. Despite the extravagant claims of the adverts, showing motorcyclists speeding towards the enemy, machine guns blazing, most of the motorcycles stayed in the US on training and internal dispatch duties.

Service in the Great War was not the first time that H-Ds and other American-built motorcycles had been used by the Armed Forces. In 1916, Indian 500 cc single-cylinder machines were on duty with the Marines at Port-Au-Prince, Haiti, and the 1000 cc Power Plus was garrisoned with 29th Marine Company in the Dominican Republic. In the spring of the same year, General Pershing went off in

search of the revolutionary Doroteo Aranga, (better known as Pancho Villa) in Mexico. He never found him, but this was the first time mechanised transport had been used by the US in the field, and it sure looked good in the H-D advertising: "Uncle Sam's Choice – Harley-Davidson." Except for a lower gear ratio, (and a Colt machine gun mounting in the sidecar, designed by Bill Harley) the motorcycles were standard, and acquitted themselves well over the rough Mexican terrain.

35 cu in, and tough.

1909 The 61 cu in 4 stroke twin, the
Sixty-One – the birth of the legend.

1910 The single gets the "pocket valve."

1914 Belt drive gives way to chain.
(The belt would actually reappear
decades later.)

1919 The company fits its own electrical
system, and more important, the export drive
begins in earnest.

Plus of course numerous modifications and improvements, competition specials and a quite extraordinary increase in production.

To point to just one statistic: under the watchful eye of William Davidson, numbers increased by some 5000% in a decade. At war's end you could buy a Harley-Davidson from a dealer in the Fiji Islands or Iceland, and one-sixth of production was going overseas, pouring out of 400,000 square feet of manufacturing space.

In 1920, single cylinder production ceased to concentrate all efforts on the bigger J model V-twins, now with battery/coil ignition. In 1919, the Sport Twin, one of the most revolutionary H-Ds ever produced, offered a horizontally opposed twin cylinder 37 cu in engine in a very light frame. It never really challenged the sporting machinery from Indian, the Scout, surviving just three years, but its very existence was a fair measure of the company's confidence.

Apart from the Sport Twin, only the Sixty-One V-twin was being produced, getting round-edged cooling fins in 1920. But despite the marvelous potential for export, the consumer rush to buy post-war, and confidence throughout the motorcycle industry, 1921 would see a tremendous slump as the economy overheated and the Ford Model T began to eat into the traditional bike market, shrinking it to the poorer working man outside the towns and the enthusiast.

As always, it would be shrewd exploitation of the V-twin that would see Harley-Davidson weather this, the first storm.

So, the horror of the Great War is over, and things are looking dandy for H-D. In 1919 a fore-head-smacking 23,000 motorcycles and 16,000 sidecars were produced. Perhaps a quick reminder of what we have seen already is in order:

1903 26 cu in single; DeDion type engine with the atmospheric inlet valve.
Not a bad start at all.

1904-1918 The "Silent Gray Fellow;"

The Heart of the Beast

Trials and Triumph for the V-Twin

"I wish to preach, not the doctrine of ignoble ease, but the doctrine of the strenuous life, the life of toil and effort."

THEODORE ROOSEVELT, CHICAGO, 1899

With production figures in 1921 about a third of what they were the previous year, and sales about a half, the plunge in confidence postwar, for H-D and other motorcycle manufacturers, was swift. The burgeoning threat from Henry Ford could perhaps have been foreseen, as his massive dealership network was put into place across the country, right alongside the H-D outlets, but it would have taken a close economic analysis of the over-expansion of US industry as a whole, (fueled partly by overlending by the banks) to predict dumping of Ford and GM models at below cost. The H-D management were not economists, they made bikes, and if the government couldn't see the looming problem, then how could they be expected to plan for this mini collapse?

H-D quickly decided to pull out of competition, partly to save money, partly to dissociate the company from the danger and vaguely "anti-social" nature of the tracks. (If you think Superbike or GP looks a dangerous way to earn a living today, you wouldn't believe the gory circus of the board tracks back then.) No one can say that the company was

not right to pull out, at a time when the H-D works riders, who had become known as the "Wrecking Crew," were at the height of their fame and success. Several of the racers transferred allegiance to Indian, who continued to support a works team: but their victories did little to halt the slow decline of the Wigwam through the decade.

Walter Davidson pledged his support to the dealers and urged them to provide better aftersales service. Arthur's overseas network of 2000 dealers in 67 countries now became a lifeline. Instead of one-sixth of production being exported, as was the case pre-war, 50% was shipped out in the early 1920s. A pointer to the success of importer Duncan Watson in the UK was the imposition in 1925 of a 33⅓% tax by the British government, anxious to protect its own beleaguered motorcycle industry.

The utility market was also essential: by 1924, 1400 police departments were riding Harley-Davidsons. A somewhat cruel but lucky break for H-D was the failure of small accessory suppliers. The company stepped into the gap, producing its own speedos, lighting sets etc. for the first time. Producing these internally not only saved money in the long run, it made money, giving the dealers something else to sell. For the first time (and not for the last) pressure was brought to bear on the dealers to ensure that they sold only official H-D extras.

If you want to know about every nut, bolt and tappet of the H-D story, something we don't have room for here, read Harry V Sucher's excellent *Harley-Davidson – The Milwaukee Marvel*. He points out a telling example of the importance of the aftersales market at this time. As the V-twin J models gained in power, the cam followers couldn't take the strain and tended to wear out. Remember that at this time, riders would often have a more intimate knowledge of their machines than they would today, and some discovered that Indian cam followers could do the job better. Stern warnings were sent out to the franchises that they were to discourage this (fairly staightforward) replacement. To change the traditional H-D valve/cam set-up would have been expensive for the company, so thicker metal was tried. But some dealers ignored the ticking off from head office, benefiting H-D's huge rival.

Cosmetically, Brewster green replaced olive drab as the standard paint scheme in 1922, but only for

LEFT **This is the reason just about everbody knows a Harley-Davidson when they see one. It has a big V-twin engine and more often than not, the owner has made it his very own, perhaps with stunning paintwork like this, perhaps just an aftermarket muffler.**

a couple of years; three coats with gold striping, varnished and baked. H-D advertising was as vigorous as ever, the aftermarket drive particularly

BELOW **The 1932 74 cu in model V, olive green with vermilion striping. The 74 cu in machines had been pocket valve from 1922, side valve from 1930 to 1936.**

RIGHT **A 1948 Police model. the year when the Knucklehead gave way to the Panhead. The push for police sales had been relentless.**

hard sell. "For Fall Driving: Sweater Coats, Windproof Vests. Ask about them … Leather helmet has caps over the ears and strap at the top which facilitates removal from the head." (Well that's a godsend.) "How far did you go yesterday? That's the first question the gang will ask you when you get back on the job Monday morning. You want to be able to tell 'em right to the dot and you want to tell 'em your highest speed too. That's just what you can do if your bus is equipped with a Corbin Speedometer. If some of the fellows doubt your word just tell 'em to to cast their lookers over your Corbin." Harley-Davidson even sent out a direct mail flyer in 1924, urging potential buyers to try a new hire purchase deal. Arthur Davidson sent super-salesman Alfred Rich Child to South Africa, where Indian were doing well, on a J with sidecar. He took over 400 orders on that extraordinary adventure, including 50 for a dictator/chief in Mombassa! Another one of Rich Child's spectacular successes was in Japan, where after a long and complex interlude (which involved distracting and essentially boring problems with exchange rates) Harley-Davidsons were actually built under license by the Sankyo company in Shinagawa. It will come as no surprise to the H-D fanatic that the Japanese motorcycle industry was born in the USA! (It's not strictly true, but it's somehow comforting.)

The company also invited all dealers to Juneau Avenue for a pep talk in the spring of 1922, where the firm financial footing of the company was described in glowing terms by the Chairman of H-D's main bank – which one would have thought

HARLEY-DAVIDSON   •   BREAKTHROUGH 3

EL "Knucklehead" 1936

Available from 1936 until 1947, (EL39 below) the "Knucklehead" engine was the precursor of today's Harley-Davidson engines.

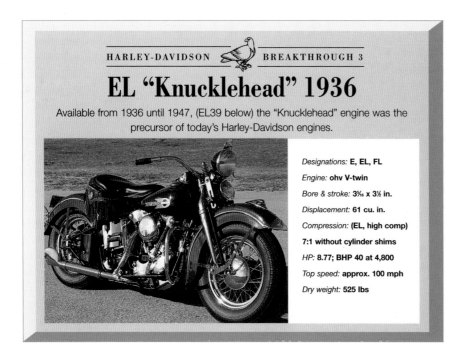

Designations: **E, EL, FL**

Engine: **ohv V-twin**

Bore & stroke: **3⁵⁄₁₆ x 3½ in.**

Displacement: **61 cu. in.**

Compression: **(EL, high comp)**

7:1 without cylinder shims

HP: **8.77; BHP 40 at 4,800**

Top speed: **approx. 100 mph**

Dry weight: **525 lbs**

would be enough to make anybody immediately look for another job.

FURTHER SPORTS EXPLORATIONS

While all this marketing, finagling with paint, selling Harley-Davidson oil and Harley-Davidson racing jerseys was going on, what was happening to the machinery? Most important, in 1922, the 74 cu in V-twin, the JD, (with pocket valve until 1929) made its debut, offered in response to the popularity of the combination, where naturally an increase in engine capacity was desirable. The Sport Twin was withdrawn after about 6000 had been built. There was nothing wrong with it, it just hadn't seriously challenged the Indian Scout, having less torque in particular. Its disappearance probably had a lot to do with William Davidson's consistent drive to rationalize production by avoiding a multiplicity of models; the author also suspects, in more general terms, that it disappeared because it wasn't a 45-degree V-twin, and therefore looked suspicious!

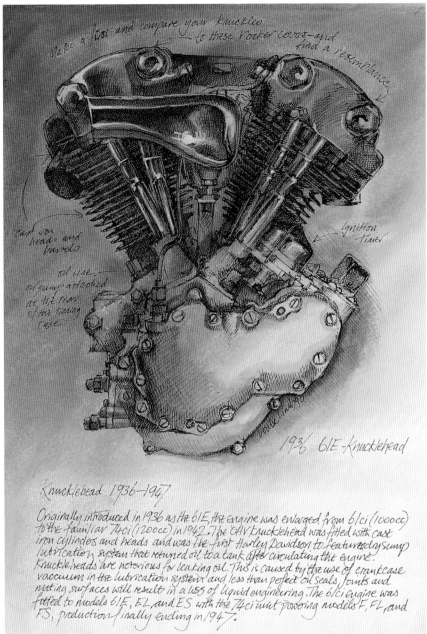

Make a list and compare your knuckles to these rocker covers—and find a resemblance

cast iron heads and barrels

oil line. oil pump attached at the rear of the timing case

Ignition timer

1936 61E-Knucklehead

Knucklehead 1936–1947

Originally introduced in 1936 as the 61E, the engine was enlarged from 61ci (1000cc) to the familiar 74ci (1200cc) in 1942. The OHV knucklehead was fitted with cast iron cylinders and heads and was the first Harley Davidson to feature a dry sump lubrication system that returned oil to a tank after circulating the engine. Knuckleheads are notorious for leaking oil. This is caused by the use of crankcase vacuum in the lubrication system and less than perfect oil seals, joints and mating surfaces will result in a loss of liquid engineering. The 61ci engine was fitted to models 61E, EL, and ES with the 74ci unit powering models F, FL, and FS, production finally ending in 1947.

One apparent gap in the market was explored, but not pursued, probably once again at the behest of William Davidson. The four-cylinder Henderson and Ace had been a best seller particularly to police departments, offering the clear advantage of less vibration than the H-D V-twin. With the Ace gone in 1924, Bill Harley brought in Everett O. DeLong (former Ace designer) to put a four-cylinder machine together. After various false starts, he placed two J-type engines side-by-side on a common crankcase to give about 80 cu in displacement with sleeved barrels. Despite having followed William's instructions that the new machine would

LEFT **The Knucklehead mill has some fanatical supporters, some of whom claim that it was the most efficient engine produced by H-D right up until the Evo, particularly in 74 cu in guise, running cooler than the later Panhead and Shovelhead.**

37

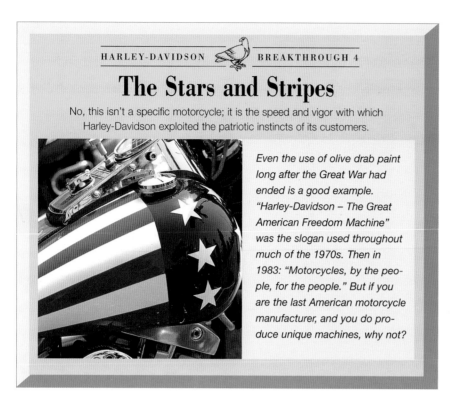

The Stars and Stripes

No, this isn't a specific motorcycle; it is the speed and vigor with which Harley-Davidson exploited the patriotic instincts of its customers.

Even the use of olive drab paint long after the Great War had ended is a good example. "Harley-Davidson – The Great American Freedom Machine" was the slogan used throughout much of the 1970s. Then in 1983: "Motorcycles, by the people, for the people." But if you are the last American motorcycle manufacturer, and you do produce unique machines, why not?

FACTORY EXPANSION

We have already mentioned the rapid expansion of H-D in the early years, from a shed, to a bigger shed, to Juneau Avenue, and of course that expansion has continued. The top building is the main plant illustrated just before US entry into the Second World War. The building (bottom) is the Butler plant acquired in fall of 1947, with 269,000 square feet of floor space. The main site is now in York, though engines are still built near Milwaukee.

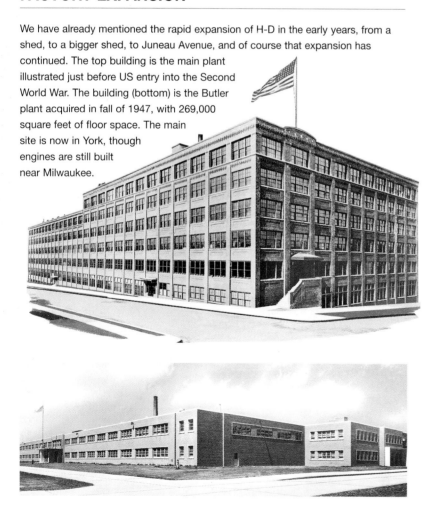

have to fit in with current production and use already available parts, William said no. Once again, although the existence of such a machine at that time opens up all kinds of intriguing possibilities for the subsequent history of the company, it looks as if he was probably right. Impossible to prove of course: but without an H-D four-cylinder motorcycle in existence, this left Henderson with a monopoly, which meant they could up the price, and they did. Where are they now? Once again, the Twin is King.

Of far more value in the long term – and a lot less expensive – was an update for the J model. To be honest, it was looking a little old by now, a spindly veteran not that different to its appearance in 1914. The frame was lowered to give a sleeker look and a lower seat, and a new, bulbous fuel tank was fitted (storing both oil and fuel). Wider, smaller-diameter tires also helped the new look. The redesign, by Arthur Constantine, was completed in 1925. "Now that's more like it!" you can almost hear William breathe a sigh of relief. "It didn't cost!" Setting aside for the moment (considered in the next chapter) the all-new Model A 21 cu in single, the "Peashooter," introduced in 1926, the next important period of change is the problematic transformation of the lineup at the end of the decade, outlined in the introduction. The new 74 cu in side valve twin, the "Flathead" VL, too heavy and with no better performance than the old J models, was sorted out just as the Wall Street Crash brought manufacturing to its knees. In 1930, the model range was cut from 13 to just six. By 1933, H-D sales would be just 3,703, the lowest since 1910. By then, Henderson had gone, (in 1931) and the next few years would be a fight for survival as the Depression bit deeper and deeper.

The fight was against a background of terrible economic hardship, but more specifically, it was against Indian. Indian found a saviour in E Paul DuPont, multimillionaire and motoring enthusiast, but H-D had no such fairy godfather and held its life in its own hands.

The work force was reduced, and those left took

BELOW The term "Special Sport Solo" was used of various larger models from 1934, including the 61, 74, and 80 cu in examples. How "Sport" is defined is not set in stone, but real sporting performance would only come with the Sportster.

a pay cut. Harley-Davidson turned to an old milch cow, the utility market, and bypassing dealerships offered the police model VL direct, practically at cost. In 1932, the Servi-Car also turned up to help cash flow.

The statistics show that H-D won the battle with Indian at this time, outselling them two to one – but it was actually even stevens at home: once again, exports were the lifeline. Despite, or perhaps, because of, the harsh economic climate, H-D paint schemes became more and more flamboyant in the early thirties.

KNUCKLEHEAD: THE MAJOR BREAKTHROUGH

By 1936, the company was strong enough to introduce what is in effect the most important Harley-Davidson ever built: the 61E, the "Knucklehead." This marvelous machine was the work of racer Joe Petrali and Hank Syvertsen from the racing department. In true H-D tradition, it retained much that had gone before, including the bore and stroke of the old J Model, but the ohv engine managed to produce twice as much power. The Knucklehead

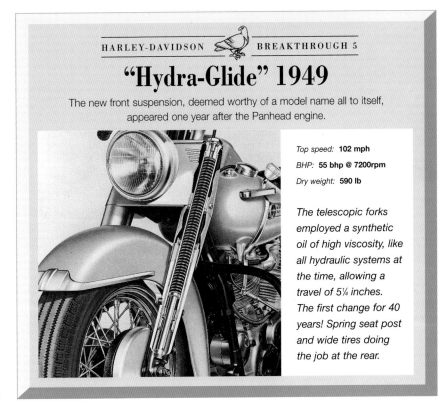

HARLEY-DAVIDSON   BREAKTHROUGH 5

"Hydra-Glide" 1949

The new front suspension, deemed worthy of a model name all to itself, appeared one year after the Panhead engine.

Top speed: **102 mph**

BHP: **55 bhp @ 7200rpm**

Dry weight: **590 lb**

The telescopic forks employed a synthetic oil of high viscosity, like all hydraulic systems at the time, allowing a travel of 5¼ inches. The first change for 40 years! Spring seat post and wide tires doing the job at the rear.

didn't turn up overnight of course: work had started back in 1931. The new valve system was the key, using unequal length push-rods operated by a single cam. The clutch was stronger, the four-speed gearbox unbreakable, the engine was slung in a double tube cradle, the forks were thicker, the top speed was about 90 then, with its tear drop tank, its oil damped, sprung saddle, the carb in the middle of the V and exhaust pipes out wide: it still does today. The total loss oil system, which often lived up to its name too quickly, was replaced with a system whereby fluctuations in crankcase pressure were manipulated to pull back oil from the heads into the crankcase. An

ABOVE **A beautifully presented Panhead Hydra Glide from the first year of production, 1949.**

ABOVE RIGHT **1954 1200 cc twin. Foot shift and hand gear had been the big news for the larger twins in 1952, as was the end of production of the 61 cu in ELs in the same year, in favor of the 74 cu in FLs.**

mph (100 quite soon). There were a few teething problems, involving oil leaks from the valve gear, but nothing as fundamental as on the old VL. Bigger rocker covers were fitted to 1938 examples. Why "Knucklehead?" Sitting astride the machine and looking down to the right, the lumps on the rocker box are supposed to look like the knuckles of a fist. "Bob Fitzsimmons had a fighting heart – so has the 1934 Harley-Davidson." If H-D had known what the nickname of their new creation was going to be, they would probably have reserved the reference to the famous boxer for a few years.

The motorcycle looked exceptionally handsome

uprated EL version offered higher compression and in 1941 the inevitable 74 F (FL and FS for sidecar) was offered, when the old Flathead 74 – which had been bored out to 80 cu in – was dropped. Even the instrument panel, with integrated speedo on the tank, was a peach. (Something must have been in the air for industrial designers in 1936, the year of

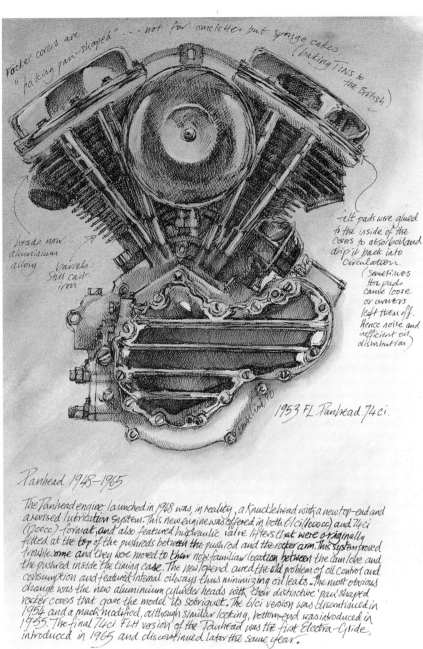

Rocker covers are "baking pan-shaped".... not for omelettes but sponge cakes. (baking Tins to the British)

heads now aluminium alloy

barrels still cast iron

Felt pads were glued to the inside of the covers to absorb and drip it back into circulation. (sometimes the pads came loose or owners left them off. Hence noise and inefficient oil distribution)

1953 FL Panhead. 74ci.

Panhead 1948-1965

The Panhead engine launched in 1948 was, in reality, a Knucklehead with a new top-end and a revised lubrication system. This new engine was offered in both 61ci (1000cc) and 74ci (1200cc) format, and also featured hydraulic valve lifters that were originally fitted at the top of the pushrods between the pushrod and the rocker arm. This system proved troublesome and they were moved to their now familiar location between the cam lobe and the pushrod inside the timing case. The new top-end cured the old problem of oil control and consumption and featured internal oilways thus minimizing oil leaks. The most obvious change was the new aluminium cylinder heads with their distinctive 'pan' shaped rocker covers that gave the model its sobriquet. The 61ci version was discontinued in 1954 and a much modified, although similar looking, bottom-end was introduced in 1955. The final 74ci FLH version of the Panhead was the first Electra-Glide, introduced in 1965 and discontinued later the same year.

the first jet aircraft, the Heinkel, the first genuine helicopter, and the immortal DC-3. Then again, it was probably the threat of war.)

The new 61 E didn't come cheap, and only just enough were sold in the first few years to justify tooling costs, but in the doughty tradition of Works Manager (and Vice-President) William A. Davidson, who died on April 21, 1937, nothing much would change in the design for the next five years. The Sixty-One Knucklehead would in fact survive until 1952.

As part of the publicity, Joe Petrali took one to Daytona and claimed the un-supercharged world

LEFT **1957 FLH, which missed out by one year on gaining a swing-arm suspension at the back. The FLH ran hotter than the FL, so was not quite so well suited as its more docile, lower compression brother for rumbling around town.**

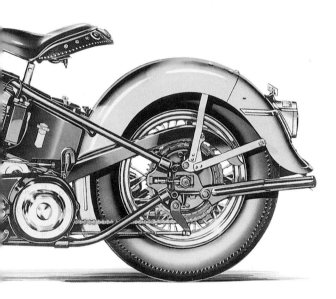

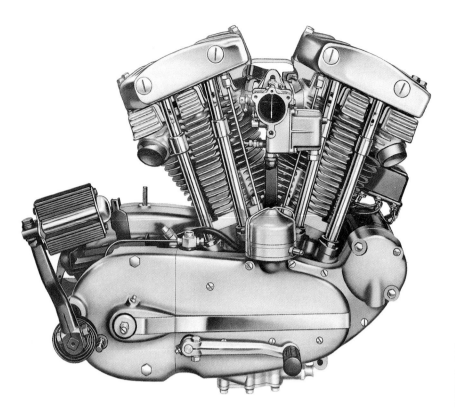

ABOVE **This is the beginning of something big: the 55 cu in engine of the 1957 Sportster, with ally pushrods and streamlined ports.**

record with a two-way average of 136.83 mph.

In the same year, police officer Fred Hamm went to what is now Edwards AFB and took the 24-hour endurance record – 1825 miles at an average speed of 76.02 mph.

What is particularly interesting, not to say satisfying, about this feat is not the bare numbers: the

record had previously been held by *four* Frenchmen. Iron Man Hamm rode alone.

As already noted, H-D had been selling to police forces almost since the company's inception – the first gas driven police vehicle in Pittsburgh, in 1909, was a Harley.

After the Second World War, the 74 FL, with low compression, was the dominant law enforcement motorcycle. The virtues specific to the products of Harley-Davidson, including the Knucklehead generation – comfortable low speed performance, bomb-proof gearboxes, plenty of power to pull extra gear – were particularly relevant to police needs.

The image of the highway patrolman on a Harley is an indelible one. The success of the big V-twins in this role would continue right up to the 1970s and the challenge from Japan, in the form of the Gold Wing flat four from Honda and the Kawasaki KZp Police Special.

The importance of this market is underlined by the fact that Kawasaki would consider it worthwhile to target a machine specifically, ensuring low maintenance costs and a low price. (H-D would

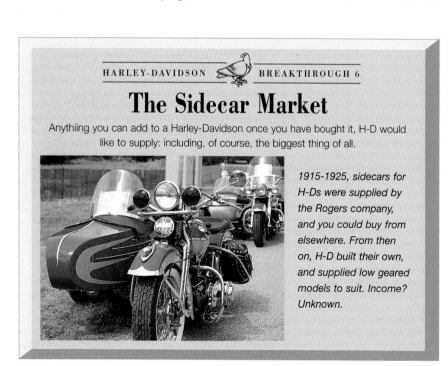

HARLEY-DAVIDSON ✦ BREAKTHROUGH 6

The Sidecar Market

Anything you can add to a Harley-Davidson once you have bought it, H-D would like to supply: including, of course, the biggest thing of all.

1915-1925, sidecars for H-Ds were supplied by the Rogers company, and you could buy from elsewhere. From then on, H-D built their own, and supplied low geared models to suit. Income? Unknown.

CENTRE **Late 1970s 74 cu incher in disguise, with a message taken to heart by quite a few H-D adherents.**

LEFT **Drilling and reaming the pump body face at the Butler plant in the 1950s, using a multiple group drill for what the literature promised would be "greater uniformity of pieces."**

BELOW **The large press for mudguards is in the background in this shot of the Butler plant; again it's the mid-1950s, but it looks like the 19th century from this distance in time.**

fight back in 1983 with the FXRTP, even modifying the fairing to meet a demand from the California Highway Patrol for 100-mph performance and undercutting the KZp on price at the expense of any worthwhile profit. By then it must have almost been a point of honor rather than a business calculation, and a question of company image.)

The Knucklehead did not hasten the end of the Flathead, which would see service for many years in 45 cu in guise; but it is fair to say that the arrival of the Knucklehead was revolutionary, and set up the company to produce the Hydra-Glide, the Electra Glide and all the other great machines, despite two more, not so fundamental engine changes – in the form of the Panhead and Shovelhead – before the 1984 second revolution. The Flathead would also survive in 74 cu in guise (now called the U series) for many years.

All of the machines tended to look similar, with the same colors and all with the recirculating oil system. The prefix "L" meant high compression, and "H" meant 80 cu in. "ULH" therefore identified a Flathead 80 cu-incher with high compression. The U, with low compression, was designed for a

TOP **The forerunner of the Sportster, the K series, this from 1953 with siamesed exhaust pipes and cow horn bars.**

ABOVE **A CH Sportster from 1959 with revised nearside engine cover.**

sidecar or some kind of cargo box to be used by, for example, the US Post Office.

The last of the Knuckleheads was produced in 1947, not such a long run for an H-D design, and some thought that its life was ended too quickly. But while the Second World War raged (H-D's involvement is outlined in the next chapter), the engineers were looking for improvements.

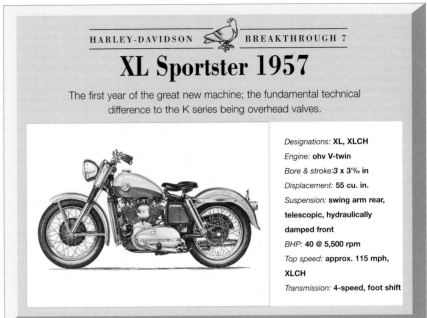

XL Sportster 1957

The first year of the great new machine; the fundamental technical difference to the K series being overhead valves.

Designations: XL, XLCH
Engine: **ohv V-twin**
Bore & stroke: **3 x 3¹³⁄₁₆ in**
Displacement: **55 cu. in.**
Suspension: **swing arm rear, telescopic, hydraulically damped front**
BHP: **40 @ 5,500 rpm**
Top speed: **approx. 115 mph, XLCH**
Transmission: **4-speed, foot shift**

PANHEAD AND HYDRA GLIDE

The biggest visible change (in 1948) was to be to the cylinder heads, capped by new rocker covers which this time were supposed to look like upside-down roasting pans; hence the unofficial nickname, the Panhead. Hydraulic valve lifters automatically took up any slack in the valvetrain, which meant that the annoying need to constantly adjust was gone. The Panhead was quieter and with aluminum heads, it ran cooler. The Panhead was a great boost to sales, with a record 32,000 of all models sold in 1949. Add-ons at the factory were numerous, such as two-tone windshields and slick mufflers.

The first H-D to come with an official name, not just a letter/number designation, was introduced in the following year. The fact that it warranted a name shows how important H-D thought the innovation was. Though "innovation" might be too strong a word.

H-D fell into line with the rest of the motorcycle world and replaced the old leading-link front suspension with telescopic forks. (No suspension at the back for a long time yet of course: no sense in mollycoddling your customer.) Foot clutch and hand shift were still the order of the day. The Hydra-Glide had all the H-D virtues, in particular presence – it was big, with fat tires and roly poly tubes over

ABOVE CENTRE **The marvelous Sportster would transform the Harley-Davidson range for ever.**

CENTRE **The Sportster H from 1965, with distinctive headlamp nacelle; very different in looks from the late 1950s Sportsters and the leaner lines of 1967.**

TOP AND ABOVE **It is interesting to compare the 1965 Sportster H (top) and the CH of 1967 side by side. Some very different styling cues are being given, from the gas tank to the mudguards.**

the front forks. The bars were rubber-mounted and adjustable, the seat was latex filled and thicker, corrosion protection was improved, the fenders were large and pretty, and for 1950, 10 bhp was added by a few tweaks. Perfect. What do you want, blood?

We are about to enter the second Golden Age of motorcycling, the 1950s. Not necessarily Harley-Davidson's best decade, but one full of wonderful smaller sporting machinery from the UK, and bikes from Harley that somehow could only have been made in the US of A, in that remarkable post-war atmosphere of confidence. An era when it seemed Uncle Sam could build – or fix – anything, including a broken Europe.

Many people (including sometimes the company's own marketing department) refer back to the

1940s as the inspiration for much of the nostalgic feel of the styling of their machines today, with some justification. However, the success of H-D as an icon for the nineties has as much to do with that remarkable early 1950s period in US history, when living standards improved rapidly for most, and the US led the world in industrial production by a street, with Europe still on its knees. Partly, this view is supported by the simple fact that many of today's H-D riders can remember the fifties from childhood – the profile of H-D owners today shows a whole slew of forty-something affluent fans, but they couldn't have remembered the bikes of the forties. What they recall (and this goes for the rest of the world maybe even more than for the domestic market) is a time when the US led the world, despite

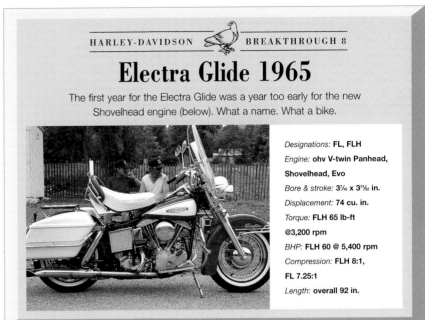

Electra Glide 1965

The first year for the Electra Glide was a year too early for the new Shovelhead engine (below). What a name. What a bike.

Designations: **FL, FLH**

Engine: **ohv V-twin Panhead,**

Shovelhead, Evo

Bore & stroke: **3⁷⁄₁₆ x 3³¹⁄₃₂ in.**

Displacement: **74 cu. in.**

Torque: **FLH 65 lb-ft**

@3,200 rpm

BHP: **FLH 60 @ 5,400 rpm**

Compression: **FLH 8:1,**

FL 7.25:1

Length: **overall 92 in.**

Chevrolet's "Triple-Turbine TurboGlide."

In July 1996 the London Sunday Times newspaper explained that "A few decades back Harleys were the preferred mode of transport for Hell's Angels gangs. It is the Angels' 'outlaw chic' that modern-day Harley owners are buying into." This gem of wisdom was offered in an article comparing the Heritage Softail with Yamaha's 1294cc Royal Star, a liquid-cooled V-four, disguised to look air-cooled, and surprisingly, nearly seven stone heavier than the 1340cc Softail. The author thinks this is plain wrong. (For a start, when did the Angels *stop* riding Harleys, as implied?) It's too glib. *Any* large motorcycle – including the Royal Star – makes a different statement to your company Toyota Corolla – but outlaw? The mature rider who chooses H-D is more often swayed by the simple fact that it is American, that it reminds him of his (fifties) childhood, and most important, that it feels very different to the H-D wannabees from Hamamatsu when you're actually in the saddle. The journalist recovered some ground by making just that point. "The Harley ... is almost animal in its feel , thrusting rider and machine forward on a shuddering wave of torque from almost zero revs. It is all so effortless and feels so good." And he is completely forgiven when he opines: "As is true in most things, the genuine article is the best. The fact that the

CENTRE A 1978 Sportster. 2,758 XLCHs were built in that year; the year in which parent company AMF began to get cold feet ...

McCarthyism, Korea, or anything else you want to point a finger at. It was a time of big industry, big plans, big bikes, a time of confidence, when for the first time to be a teenager meant something. It is fair to say that a large part of the love shown by so many for a Harley-Davidson today is a reflection of a love for 1950s America. In 1945 the US had $26 billion worth of factories that had not existed in 1940, and most of them could be converted to civilian production without too much trouble. With six percent of the world's population, by the mid-1950s, America was producing and consuming 40 percent of total global output! "Hydra-Glide" has a wonderful period feel about it, born a few years before the Thunderbird's "Trigger-Torque Power," Chrysler's "Powerflite Range-Selector" and

Yamaha is a fake does not bother a lot of riders, but it most definitely bothers Yamaha. Japanese factories usually emblazon their logos across their products. But not this time. You have to look very close to confirm that the Star is indeed a Yamaha."

The mention of outlaws introduces a very sensitive topic with H-D top brass. Harley-Davidson has always been acutely conscious of non-motorcycling public opinion – witness the decent muffler on the "Silent Gray Fellow," and the on-off affair with racing, characterised once by a hasty retreat. The company flirted once with the bad boy image, in 1987, with a photograph of some Angels – or Bandidos, or Mongols, or out-of-work actors – above the line: "Would you sell an unreliable motorcycle to these guys?" The ad came in for some heavy criticism, not least from the enthusiast, older non-"bike" H-D riders. But for most of its history, the company's marketing has laid the stress on clean-cut, outdoor fun. "Over the hills and far away! Up hill and down dale … The healthful fresh air on your cheek … Come on, let's go!" (1930.)

H-D were all in favor of the "full Dresser" look, with their machines having all the right (factory issue) bits and bobs attached, and frowned upon the new craze for "chopping." Custom "bobbers," motorcycles stripped down to the bare essentials, had been created by returning GIs, influenced perhaps by the faster, smaller machinery they had encountered overseas. The chopper look developed from them, and would be perfected in the 1960s, with longer XA and VL springer forks, 21-in front and 16-in rear wheels, solo seats, upswept fishtail pipes and apehangers, before the look was exaggerated into parody in the 1970s.

Have you ever heard of the films *Cyclist's Raid* and *Hot Blood*? You have actually, because they were alternative titles for producer Stanley Kramer's and director Laslo Benedik's *The Wild One*. starring Marlon Brando, Lee Marvin and Mary Murphy. This 1953 film was based very loosely on a 1947 rumble at Hollister, Ca. It was quite an event, involving some irate townsfolk, some bikers – and eventually, 500 lawmen! The teenage menace

OPPOSITE, ABOVE
FLT Tour Glide Classic, on display at the beginning of the 1980s, a "full Dresser."

OPPOSITE, CENTRE
The Chopper movement became more and more extreme, and reached a peak in the mid 1970s. Pegs, custom gas tank and those long "springer" forks all compulsory.

OPPOSITE, BELOW
Beautiful example of a 1968 Electra Glide. With all that kit, you can see why the few extra horses offered by the Shovelhead engine over the Panhead were put to good use.

LEFT The 1974 FXE Super Glide; Willie G's brainchild and a superb looking cruiser.

was set in the country's psyche. For the first time, the young bucks had money; and there were a lot of them. Between 1946 and 1960, the number of teenagers as a percentage of the population would double. We are not going to speculate about the outlaw connection and H-D, for fear of Milwaukee censure as much as a visit from some aggrieved chapter of the Angels! But it's there, and events in Denmark (Denmark!) in 1996, involving rival biker gangs, stolen missile launchers and murder, show that it's still there. Suffice to say that there is an incredible irony in the existence of a relationship between one of the most conservative corporations in America and the bad guys.

With the arrival of the Hydra-Glide, time for another recap.

1919-1922. The ill-fated 37 cu in horizontally opposed four-stroke twin, the Sport Twin, designation W, WJ. A good motorcycle, but not enough "Sport,"(being slower than the equivalent from Indian) and not enough "Twin," (as a non V). The Sixty-One lasts until 1929, having changed from the 1909 F to the J.

1922-1929. The pocket valve 74 cu in, the JD.

1930-1936. The side valve 74 cu in, the V and VL.

1937-1941. The 80 cu in side valve twin, the UH and ULH, benefiting from the improvements in the frame, etc. of the Knucklehead.

In addition, there had been the 21 cu in Peashooter, the 30.5 cu in "Baby Harley," the 1947 single-cylinder two stroke "Hummer", and the long-lived Forty-Five/Servi-Car, all considered in the next chapter.

In 1952 a foot gear was introduced on the Panhead, and in 1954 you got a special airhorn and

RIGHT **A 1977 Limited Edition Electra Glide Classic. As individuality was always so important to H-D customers, it made sense for the company to release exclusive runs like this.**

BELOW **It was only on the FXE 1200 in 1974 that electric start was first offered on the FX series, which had first been introduced in 1971. The buckhorn bars were an important FX styling cue.**

other delights for the Jubilee – "Fifty years – American Made" – the celebrations inexplicably a year late.

We have said that the 1950s was not actually a great decade for H-D, it just feels like it from a distance of forty years, and this is validated by the sales figures comparison for 1949 and 1955: 24,000 plays 9500. But the company was certainly still turning a profit, despite the British invasion of middleweights from AJS & Matchless, Norton and Triumph. Here was another one of the Hog's nine lives, and the escape was the same – the unique, big V-twin. The model K and 55 cu in KH was supposed to challenge in the middleweight division, but it never did in any big numbers. It wasn't the end of the world; as the eventual failure of the Arrow and Scout was for Indian.

The doors would close in 1953. In 1949, Indian had returned to its single-storey factory in Springfield, the founders' original building, the more easily to produce vertical twins and singles, 440 and 220cc respectively, and then the 500cc Warrior in 1950. Clear then, the target for Indian – that ever expanding middleweight sector. The final cruel irony is that the Indian Chief (now 80 cu in) was as good as ever, but only about 1300 were produced in the final two years, while the smaller machines flopped, with only about 500 verticals ever built. Farewell to the Hendee Manufacturing Company/Indian Motocycle [sic] Company, and hail to the Chief.

THE GREAT DIVIDE

The next great leap forward was born out of the relative failure of the KH and would divide H-D products (excluding the many smaller machines) into two strands for ever. A division, very roughly defined, between performance and top speed, and the traditional tourer. By now, there was a second generation at the helm: John Harley, product engineer, Walter C Davidson, secretary, William H Davidson, vice-president, and William J Harley, treasurer and chief engineer. In 1957 they would oversee the introduction of the 55 cu in Sportster; the division was between this model and its descendants, and the Glides.

They kept the best assets of the KH, such as unit construction and four single-lobe cams, increased the bore and provided ohv. The new XL – X following the U and V Flathead sequence – gained higher compression in the following year (as the XLH); then the real winner arrived, the XLCH, a lightened Sportster with peanut tank, alloy wheels, magneto ignition and lower gearing. The CH was supposed to stand for "Competition Hot," but it's never been confirmed. At 883cc, it ducked under the 900cc insurance band, which made it all the more attractive. The light alloy domed pistons, new rocker box and light pushrods could provide some respectable quarter-mile times. (The Sportster's foot shift, incidentally, was on the right side, unlike on the FL's.)

RIGHT **FXRS Super Glide II of 1982, with a new frame, five speeds and revised suspension.**

BELOW LEFT **The same year saw the great, belt driven 80 cu in FXB Sturgis. It used the same dual tanks and tank-mounted instrument panel as the Fat Bob model.**

BELOW RIGHT The FXWE **Wide Flide was introduced in 1980, with a 21-in front wheel, extended forks and wider triple yokes.**

The British Nortons still had better suspension, but that old H-D torque was enough to persuade more than two thousand to part with their money in the first year, a flying start. Meanwhile, the Hydra-Glide became the Duo-Glide, the solid rear end replaced by swinging arm suspension. High-speed instability was soon fixed by an adjustment to the steering head.

It was in 1960 that H-D found a way to penetrate the lightweight and middleweight sector more effectively than Indian, by tying up with the Italian Aermacchi company. They had 250s and 175s already in production – farewell to the vast expense of tooling up.

The Sprint and other models sold in big numbers through the 1960s, helping to double production figures, 1964-65. The marriage wasn't exactly made in heaven, with build quality problems and a reluctance on the part of some dealers to get behind the smaller machines – lower margins – at the expense of the FLs, FLHs and Sportsters. But the divorce,

coming as late as 1978, was amicable. And the sales of the Sprint must be considered against the background of fantastic competition form Japan.

To return to the heart of the beast: in 1962, the legendary Willie G Davidson joined the company as Director of Styling, in time to see the Duo-Glide get better brakes. In 1965, another legend turned up, and another machine deemed worthy of its own official name. The Electra-Glide (hyphen soon dropped) had twelve-volt electrics and push button start, plus a sealed primary chain. The FLH 74 cu in with highway package was the biggest motorcycle you could buy. Following the buy-in to plastics

technology at the Tomahawk Boat Company, you could even get a very cool fiberglass sidecar to go with it. (You could also buy an H-D golfcart from the same source!) In the words of the gangster anti-hero in *Goodfellas*, it had it all.

SHOVELHEAD

Well, not quite. The old Panhead was finding it heavy going hauling around all this extra weight, and in 1966, the third generation of big V-twin was introduced, offering at least 5 bhp more, which sounds more if you say ten percent. The Shovelhead vibrated less and featured a Tillotson diaphragm carburetor and new "power pac" head design. The rocker arms pivoted on shafts which led to castings on the heads, looking, apparently, like the back of a coal shovel. Accurate or no, it's a great name for a big motorcycle mill. The costs of the redesign are impossible to gauge, but whatever they were, in 1965, Harley-Davidson found it necessary to go public with its stock for the first time.

Eventually, at the beginning of 1969, a massive partner emerged: the sporting goods manufacturer

ABOVE **The 1980 Wide Glide flame paint was from the factory, along with the widely spaced fork tubes, the forward mounted foot pegs and the Fat Bob tank.**

RIGHT **80 cu in FXS Low Glide. The Low Glide would still be in production in 1985, when it would get belt drive.**

American Machine and Foundry. The merits of this "merger," which was really a takeover in all but name, have been endlessly debated by H-D cognoscenti. One thing is certain: AMF invested a great deal of money in its new partner, particularly in plant and machinery, sums of money which would have been impossible to raise if H-D had stood alone through the 1970s.

Production numbers don't tell the whole story – production is not a sure indicator of profit by any means – but in 1970 29,000 machines came out of Milwaukee, in 1971 37,000, in 1972 just shy of 60,000 and in 1973 71,000. With AMF's York, Pennnsylvania factory converted for motorcycle output, by then production capacity had been quadrupled. AMF "bought" H-D from its stockholders by exchanging $21,650,000 of its own stock for all H-D assets.

Which is of course a meaningless statistic. H-D's assets were only worth whatever people motorcyclists thought of the next model, and whether the traditional H-D riders would keep the faith. The Sportster held its own against all-comers right through the sixties, but by then some of the bigger British machines were beginning to challenge; and Honda's in-line four CB750 of 1969, with a top speed around 123 mph, was seriously bad news.

The Sportster got a fiberglass boat-tail one-piece seat for 1970, and the Shovelhead got an AC generator to replace the old DC unit, which meant some were plunged into mourning for the passing of the old backup kick start.

SPECIAL FX

These were not, however, the most important changes at the beginning of the decade. Alongside the expansion of the list of smaller capacity models, Willie G Davidson came up with a wonderful idea. With the chopper movement in full swing, it made no sense to ignore what people plainly wanted. He took the frame and powerplant of the FL and married it to the front of the XL, to create the FX 1200 Super Glide. Footpegs, not boards, no starter

motor, longer aluminum forks for that vital laid-back look.

Why was it such a good idea? Well, on the one hand you have the FL big tourer, a safe option and fully "dressed" in 1969 with bar-mounted fairing and large fiberglass saddlebags. Nowhere much to go with that. On the other, you have the Sportster, under pressure in terms of performance from Europe (including Germany and Italy) and Japan. Ok, give it 61 cu in (1972) but again, there's not a lot you can do.

Combine the two, and you avoid direct comparisons with the speedier competition, but you provide more speed than the big tourers while retaining their ability to pooter around town. In effect, you do what Soichiro Honda said he always did: "We do not service the market. We create the market." With the Super Glide, H-D had invented a niche which simply hadn't been there before. Brilliant.

Electric start an option in 1974, 108 mph and 560 lb weight, the perfect compromise, without any of the pitfalls which compromise can bring. The hybrid handled extremely well. Soon FXs were outselling Sportsters.

At this point federal regulations began to bite, but AMF had the money to develop the Ham Can air filter and fit a big 10-in front disc brake to the Electra Glide. (The 55-mph limit was instituted in

BELOW **A 1974 XL1000 on display in London, England, proudly flying the flag for AMF.**

XLCR "Café Racer" 1977

No turkey of course, except in sales terms.
Just a styling experiment that did not catch on.

Designation: **XLCR**

Engine: **ohv V-twin**

Bore & stroke: **3⁵⁄₁₆ x 3½ in.**

Displacement: **1000 cc**

Body: **bikini fairing, angular tank, two-into-two siamesed exhaust headers**

Frame: **Lightweight triangulated space type**

Production: **3,123**

Willie also introduced the XLCR Cafe Racer: "Only one man could have done this ... it couldn't have been built by a committee" boasted the advertising copy. Unfortunately not many more than one wanted to buy it. The bikini fairing, the slab-sided fuel tank, solo seat and siamesed two-into-two exhaust headers, good grief, even the black paint – it all seemed to fit the cafe racing image which was all the rage.

ABOVE **Close-up on the 1978 Sportster engine, with ignition switch above the large chromed horn in the middle of the cylinders.**

1974.) In 1977 Willie G developed the FX concept with the FXS Low Rider, predating the 1997 Yamaha Drag Star rather neatly by exactly twenty years.

As one commentator said of the Drag Star "If you're going to copy something you might as well go the whole Hog." The Low Rider, surprise, had shortened suspension; plus a scooped seat which held the rider just 27 inches from the road. The drag-type bars also helped the low, sleek look and were also probably a boon to female riders, along with the low riding position.

Why was nobody buying? Well, it was the old story. If I want to buy a Harley-Davidson, I want to buy a Harley-Davidson. If I want a road racer, I'll look elsewhere. The XLCR lasted just two years. (It's a collectible classic today, of course.)

1978 was H-D's 75th birthday, and true to form they celebrated with a limited edition XL-1000 Sportster, (gold trim and leather saddle). 1978 was also the swan song for the lower compression FL.

1980 was a good year; not because Ronald Reagan was elected President, but because there were three new Harley-Davidsons. (Well, two and a bit, and one was actually first built at the end of 1979.) The FLT Tour Glide was a very distinctive looking machine, with twin headlights on the fairing, and the steering head in front of the fork crowns. Five speeds for the first time on a V-twin, which was set up to reduce vibration. You have to

LEFT **XLH from 1978. The squared air box wasn't a popular change.**

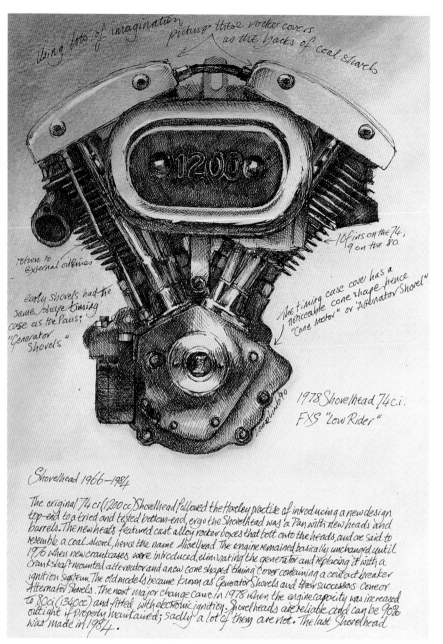

Using lots of imagination picture these rocker covers as the backs of coal shovels

return to external oillines

early shovels had the same shape timing case as the Pans; "Generator Shovels"

←10 fins on the 74, 9 on the 80.

The timing case cover has a noticeable cone shape hence "Cone motor" or "Alternator Shovel"

1978 Shovelhead 74 c.i. FXS "Low Rider"

Shovelhead 1966-1984

The original 74 ci (1200 cc) Shovelhead followed the Harley practise of introducing a new design top-end to a tried and tested bottom-end, ergo the Shovelhead was a Pan with new heads and barrels. The new heads featured cast alloy rocker boxes that bolt onto the heads, and one said to resemble a coal shovel, hence the name Shovelhead. The engine remained basically unchanged until 1970 when new crankcases were introduced, eliminating the generator and replacing it with a crankshaft mounted alternator and a new cone shaped timing cover containing a contact breaker ignition system. The old models became known as Generator Shovels and their successors Cone or Alternator Shovels. The next major change came in 1978 when the engine capacity was increased to 80 ci (1340 cc) and fitted with electronic ignition. Shovelheads are reliable and can be 90% outright if properly maintained; sadly a lot of them are not. The last Shovelhead was made in 1984.

"Hugger"), in 1980 you could also buy the latest offspring of the FX union, the glorious FXB Sturgis. This really was a looker, and still is. Extended forks, buckhorn bars, stepped seat, lots of black paint highlighted in orange. What was technically interesting was the use of aramid fiber belts for both primary (engine to transmission) and secondary (transmission to rear wheel) drive. They were long lasting and reduced transmission backlash: remember that was one of the plusses of belts when they were phased out right at the beginning of this story! Top speed was about 108 mph from the 80 cu in Shovelhead. I want one.

Also new, the FXWG Wide Glide, was a Fat Bob with a bobbed rear fender: in the end, you just can't help writing a ridiculous sentence like that, as the numbers and letters get all mixed up with the names, and your brain turns to mush. The Fat Bob (1979) was essentially a Super Glide with things stripped off, but retaining the big dual fuel tanks. Bobbed, but still fat, got it? Now, the Wide Glide had wider triple clamps , a spoked 21-in front wheel … let's just forget it and say that all the FXs at this time are the results of the efforts of Willie G and President Vaughn Beals to second-guess the customisers; and they're all successful.

The AMF era is now drawing to a close; the legacy was enormous. In 1979, the company could easily produce 50,000 motorcycles and ten years earlier the figure had been around 15,000. Smaller capacity machines, built in Italy and in the US, had sold in respectable numbers (more in the next chapter). There had been complaints about build quality on these machines and on some of the big V-twins, electrical problems and oil leaks being the most common.

AMF itself wanted to divest itself of the company, as manufacturing costs soared and the expected return on the capital investment did not materialise. It is difficult to analyse such a complicated matter in a short space, but the most obvious explanation of why AMF felt that its investment had been a failure, is that its aim had been impossible from the very beginning.

admit that it had taken a long, long time for H-D to do anything much about the inherent vibration problems of their particular configuration, except providing nice thick bar grips! The "Tri-Mount" setup allowed the engine, transmission and swinging arm to be suspended in the frame and isolated by three rubber mounting points. Two ball-joint stabilisers allowed lateral movement. The subsequent reduction in vibration was a genuine advance, as were the three disc brakes and the increase of the fuel tank capacity to five gallons.

Alongside the XLS (extended forks) and the XLH (lower seat, and shorter shocks, the

In effect, it took what it considered to be an outdated manufacturing setup and tried to turn it into a huge, mass production industry, with the economies of scale that entails. The simple fact is, a large capacity Harley-Davidson motorcycle can never be a truly mass produced item, partly because it is too complex, but more importantly, because there aren't a "mass" of people who actually want it, at whatever price or in whatever condition! Their statement was brief: "AMF have failed to make the company a going concern." But with AMF tired of trying to achieve the impossible, this was by no means the end of the H-D adventure, as it could have been; the Hog still has a few lives left.

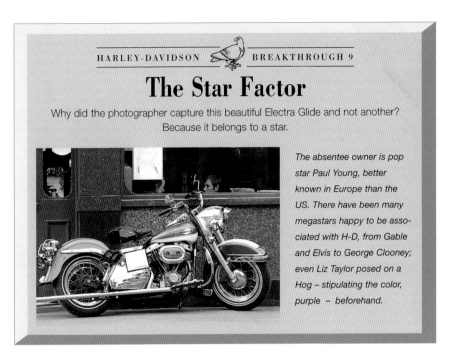

The Star Factor

Why did the photographer capture this beautiful Electra Glide and not another? Because it belongs to a star.

The absentee owner is pop star Paul Young, better known in Europe than the US. There have been many megastars happy to be associated with H-D, from Gable and Elvis to George Clooney; even Liz Taylor posed on a Hog – stipulating the color, purple – beforehand.

LEFT **Glides lined up at Daytona Beach in the 1970s. To work out the exact date, it might be helpful to check the cars as well as the Hog engines …**

'Baby' Brothers

The Undulating Fortunes of the Little Harleys

*In the complicated agitation of modern existence,
our wearied souls dream of simplicity.*

CHARLES WAGNER, THE SIMPLE LIFE

In the very early years (see chapter one) the single cylinder machines were of course dominant, the 50 cu in 6.5 hp twin, the Model 5D, first appearing in 1909. H-D is famous today, and has been from about 1918 and the 61 cu in Model 18J, for large capacity V-twin machines. But there has been a profusion of smaller capacity motorcycles since then (none today), the most important of which is the Forty Five.

Before examining the long history of that doughty workhorse and warhorse, there is one single which deserves closer attention, the 1926-34 Peashooter. In 1925, Cleveland phased out their lightweight, and both H-D and Indian tried to step into the gap, the Indian with a 21 cu in side valve, the "Prince." H-D went one better, producing two 21 cu in models, the "A," and the ohv "AA," capable of a sprightly 65-mph top speed. The best sales were in Europe, not at home, as was often the case for the smaller H-Ds. In this case, the economical running was the key. At 18 cents a gallon, huge distances for loose change didn't cut much ice at home, but it was a deciding factor abroad where gas was much more expensive. With its high power-to-

weight ratio, it was a natural for the flat tracks of Australia, New Zealand and Great Britain, and with the magnificent racer Joe Petrali aboard, it dominated the new 21 cu in class on the short tracks at home.

During the same period, another challenge was set by a rival manufacturer, this time not by withdrawing a model, but by introducing one. Excelsior surprised everyone by introducing the "Super X," a 45 cu in middleweight with H-D type pocket valve, and in-unit construction of the engine and gearbox. H-D set to work on their own 45-incher, and a comparison of their machine with the Super X highlights once again all of the time-honored H-D virtues. The Super X had good performance, and was techincally more advanced, (ie, not side valve) but its components were not as sturdy, particularly the lower bearing assembly. The Flathead 45, after some teething problems (quite literally, the 32-tooth rear sprocket quickly replaced with 28 at the same time as the compression was increased) was here to stay, unlike the Super X.

Following the Wall Street Crash the Forty Five was reintroduced with a new frame and new front fork in 1930. After that, there was a gradual improvement of the basic machine year on year, through various model designations, right up until the Second World War. Ground clearance was increased. a new single headlamp was fitted in place of the twin lamps of the early models. In 1932 the designation was the Model R, and the generator

LEFT **US Army riders and mechanics were given instruction on the maintenence of their Forty Fives with the use of cutaway engines like this one.**

was moved to the front of the engine. There was heavier gauge tubing, aluminum pistons in 1934, the brakes were upgraded in 1936, a new oil pump in 1937, the clutch was strengthened for 1938 and a big-twin type rocking clutch pedal was fitted. In 1941, it was the clutch again, with a larger hub and two fiber discs, one spring disc, together with strengthened gears and stronger brakes. Which leads us to the Forty Five's finest hour.

ABOVE LEFT **What dominates from this angle on the early DL engine is the generator in front of the cylinders. The DL was known as the "three-cylinder" Harley because of this.**

LEFT **This 1930 DL is on display at Max Middlebosch's motorcycle museum in Zwolle, Holland.**

HARLEY-DAVIDSON IN THE SECOND WORLD WAR

There is one motorcycle on these pages which might stand out: the combination (bottom right) is of course not a Harley-Davidson. But it is not pictured just as an example of what the Japanese were producing in opposition to the Forty Five. From as early as the First World War, H-Ds had been imported into Japan. In 1929 the value of the yen plummeted, but rather than give up the lucrative market, H-D allowed the Sankyo company to build motorcycles under license, using H-D blueprints and metallurgical expertise. Built as the "Rikuo," roughly translated as "king of the road," and based upon the VL side valve Harley, the motorcycles became the Type 97 Military model from 1937. About 18,000 were built between 1937 and 1942.

The other pictures on these pages have been chosen to indicate the wide reach of the WLA, put into service not just by the US Army and Marines, but also by various Allied forces, including the RAF and the Canadian Army.

LEFT **Pvt. Wilburn L Cummings gets to know hisWLA in England. The leading link forks are about to be tested. (Imperial War Museum)**

BELOW **Another famous picture, at a US training camp in Australia. Apparently, according to the accompanying fanfare, he was off, Tommy gun ready, in 3 seconds.**

ABOVE **A 1942 WLC with the Canadian Provost Corps.**

OPPOSITE, BELOW **The RAF make use of a WLC in France. The convoy is about to leave Creully. (IWM)**

BELOW **Abandoned Sankyo Type 97, following recapture of Dutch barracks at Balikapapan, Borneo. (AWM 305117)**

RIGHT **John McKenna from Fayetteville, New York, looks pretty pleased with this WLA – as well he should be. It came from the US Army and had been in storage for 40 years, undisturbed!**

in that the Forty Fives (and other machines) were capable of taking the battering of a war zone without breaking down, and right, in that there was no need for more power or performance than the Forty five offered. In the summer of 1939, President Roosevelt announced that American industry should gear up to assist the Allies; by the end of the conflict, the US would have supplied more than $42 billion worth of equipment to 44 countries under Lend-Lease, Great Britain and the USSR the main recipients.

"CRY 'HAVOC!' AND LET SLIP THE HOGS OF WAR"

In November 1938, Bill Harley attended a Quartermaster Corps motorcycle reliability conference at Camp Holabird in Baltimore, and returned with an order for 2000 military motorcycles. As explained in chapter one, H-D were no strangers to military procurement, having supplied more than 7,000 machines for the Great War, and sold motorcycles for military application to other nations between the wars.

In December 1928, !st Lt. Vernon Megee of the US Marine Corps wrote in the Marine Corps Gazette: "The modern motorcycle … will not stand up under service conditions. The machines now in use are far more powerful than is necessary for solo work; they are in fact dangerous in the hands of any but an expert rider. Several serious accidents have occurred in the 3rd Brigade [in China] due to the use of these heavy machines in traffic." He went on to recommend the use of smaller, less powerful motorcycles for expeditionary forces. Motorcycle technology had come on apace since then of course, and by 1941, he was both right and wrong. Wrong,

Even as the President was setting out his stall that summer, preparing the country to enter the conflict directly, Indian were building 5000 Chief sidecar outfits for the French army. H-D were preparing 5000 solo machines for Great Britain, following the bombing of the Triumph factory in Coventry. Under either government contract or Lend-Lease Harley-Davidson would supply something like 88,000 machines, with substantial numbers shipped to Canada, Great Britain, South Africa, Russia and China.

The reorganization of the US Army, which included mechanization sorely needed even at such a late date (the US having cut military expenditure in the thirties, as had the allies) allowed for cavalry reconnaissance squadrons to run ahead of the new five divisions. The recce squadrons would use scout cars and motorcycles, both solo and with sidecars.

The majority of H-Ds (probably 60,000-plus, though exact figures are impossible to ascertain) were supplied to the US forces; and most of those were the WLA Forty Five.

LEFT **The teardrop shaped tool box was fitted to the WLA from 1940 onward. Everything on this machine is exactly factory spec.**

Such an internationally famous and well-loved motorcycle deserves a full specification breakdown:

1939, 740cc, 69.85 x 96.85mm.
Compression ratio 6:1
23 hp at 4500 rpm, single Schebler carb, 6v,
    coil ignition
Hand-change, three-speed, right foot
    kick start
Tubular frame, duplex cradle
Leading link, helical sprung, friction damped
    front suspension
Internal expanding drum brakes,
    front and rear
4 x 18-in tires, front and rear

Overall length 88 in, height 41 in
Unladen weight 535 lb (242 kg)
Fuel tank 12.5 litres
Range 119 miles, top speed 60 mph
Military equipment: rear carry rack, leather

RIGHT **A brass date plate on a 1942 WLA. "Parts list TM-10-1482 ... Do not exceed 65 m.p.h."**

panniers, crash bars front and rear, a scabbard for a Thompson sub-machine gun or rifle mounted on the right front fork, crank case guard, service livery with black exhaust system, military air filter on carb for desert conditions.

The robustness of the WLA is evidenced by the survival of many still being ridden in Europe today. They were sold as war surplus, sometimes for as little as $25, a very real peace dividend for the canny. These surplus machines were often stripped down and fitted with aftermarket parts, thus fueling the

LEFT **This XA has
several standard US
Army parts such as the
ammunition box and
military lights.**

customizing trend of the 1950s. The WLC, supplied to Canadian forces, had different rear lights as specified by the Canadian Army and an additional carrier box on the front fender, among other details.

For those machines that actually did get shipped abroad, what role did they play?

The image of the machine gunner charging across country on his trusty iron is a very seductive one, and some motorcyclists did support armored divisions in battle.

"The mounts of the Rough Riders, toughest and fastest of land army troops," as they were described by *This Week* magazine in 1942. But for the most part, the Forty Five was ridden by scouts, by MPs, by military "traffic cops," able to guide the huge troop movements, by those on general liaison duties, couriers – and by troops just moving from area to another. (There is a consistent story that says 30,000 Russians rode west through Eastern Germany on Harley-Davidsons in the final push for Berlin, but the production figures don't quite add up to that many. Though it is certainly true that H-Ds *did* enter Berlin from both "fronts.")

The WLA was carried horizontally by the armored division tanks, 540 per division, and was found to be none the worse for the rough handling.

NECESSITY AS THE MOTHER OF IMITATION

Alongside limited numbers of the big V-twins, (for example, some 670 of the 1200 cc UA – A for Army – to the US Army and more to British forces in South Africa), Harley-Davidson also supplied an interesting flat twin 45 with shaft drive. The XA was specifically requested by the US Army Procurement Authorities. The Allies had noted the success of the German BMW R75s and Zundapp KS750s, particularly in the deserts of North Africa. H-D took a BMW R12, pulled it apart and more or less copied it. Four speeds, side valve engine, two carbs, unit construction, plunger-type rear suspension, and most important, it was a transverse flat twin. Only about 1,000 were built, not because the design was particularly flawed but because the war had moved on, for the US in particular, to the Pacific theater, where the Jeep was king.

There were eight main American-built motorcycles in military service, which were specifically modified

for the forces, in the Second World War. Plus one that didn't quite make it. Three of them were H-Ds: the WLA, the XA and the ELA, similar to the UA but with a smaller 1000 cc engine, and used mostly for sidecar escort, and MP duties.

The non-runner was the 90-degree twin 45 cu in Indian Model 841, again developed at the request of the army, with shaft drive. 1056 were built, but the contract was terminated and none were ever shipped out.

Indian were really unlucky on this occasion: thirty years later, Moto Guzzi would produce a motorcycle with the same design, including the duplex cradle frame, the girder type forks – the V7 – but with a more powerful ohv engine, which was considered ideal for military service.

The Indian Chief, the 340B, was supplied in numbers to the US forces and to the allies. Indian also developed and supplied the 640A, a 500 cc model based on the Sport Scout, and the 45 cu in 640B. At least 18,000 of the former were built, a respectable number but nowhere near Harley-

BELOW **The Forty Five was always supposed to have sufficient power to haul a sidecar. Some versions were lower geared for that purpose.**

RIGHT **In 1941, H-D introduced the WR, a Class C racer. The engine had larger valves than the standard WL, and the later WRs had magneto drive.**

availability of war surplus WLAs helped to spread the word for H-D, and full-scale civilian production would recommence in 1947, once the supply of raw materials was restored.

The side valve 45 soldiered on until 1952, to be replaced by the K model, still 45 cu in and side valve, but with unit construction, four speeds, hand shift/foot clutch. Wiilliam H Davidson viewed the K as a stopgap machine, on the road to the Sportster dynasty. There were problems, particularly with the gears, and the K wasn't really a performer when put up against the British opposition, even when upped

Davidson's prodigious output. Two other machines are worth a brief mention, because of their unusual nature.

The Servi-Cycle was supplied by Simplex of New Orleans to the USAF, its 165 lb weight made it a practical mode of transport for airborne troops over short distances. The Cushman Autoglide was supplied by one of the Johnson-Evinrude divisions in Lincoln, Nebraska: remember Mr Ole Evinrude had been a useful advisor to the founders of H-D back in 1903, and had since made his name with marine engines. This air droppable machine had a 2544 cc engine and tiny 6.00 x 6-in tires.

WINNING THE PEACE

Just after the death of William S Harley in September 1943, the US Army cancelled an order for 1105 H-Ds. They had seen that they were in fact over-supplied, and that four-wheel transport was more effective in most scenarios. But that wasn't the end of the Forty Five story by a long way. The

to 55 cu ins in 1954. There are two other parts to the Forty Five story, one of which is discussed in the following chapter, the WRs in competition. The second is the remarkable success and longevity of the Servi-Car.

Introduced in 1932, it was, according to company literature, "intended primarily for use by garages and service stations in the pickup and delivery of customers' cars." The back wheels were 42 inches apart, which meant that the rider could follow the tracks of a car through mud or snow. The idea was that one man rode out to the vehicle to be serviced,

hooked up the Servi-Car with a standard tow bar and drove the car to the station. The Servi-Car certainly was used in this way, but most of the sales were actually to traffic police.

The reason it lasted so long (until 1974, when just 70 were sold, as the utility auto finally won out) was that it was all of a piece.

The frame was not just an add-on box lashed to a Forty Five, but specifically engineered. It was cheap to run, easy to ride, stable, and didn't need too much servicing. The fact that you could buy a new one right up until 1974 is fairly astonishing.

LEFT **1975 SS250, engine very similar to the Yamaha DT-1. Two strokes were getting a very bad press from the environmental lobby at the time, which didn't help sales.**

UTILITY MOTORCYCLES

The Forty Five, having transformed itself through no less than ten designations from 1929 to 1952, left behind a legacy which would survive until 1974. The Servi-Car was bought for the most part by police forces, but there were some other utility applications for the dependable side valve, both in three-wheeler and conventional form. The Dutch roadside repair service, for example, started up again post-war on 25 WLCs. The Servi-Car was the first H-D with electric start (1964, pre Electra G).

FAR LEFT **The box was 29 in wide, 23 in long, a foot high, first steel then later fiberglass. Perfect for tools, ice cream maybe, and today, a picnic.**

LEFT AND BELOW LEFT **The "Liberator," as it was known in Europe, put to work after the war by the Dutch roadside repair service, the ANWB. The box is actually a recycled airdrop cannister. Restorer Roel Donatz even has the right period clothing.**

TOP **1955 GE Servi-Car. Owner John Hessels found the Semo Motor Patrol logo under layers of paint in the course of a restoration, and decided to keep it.**

ABOVE **1934 model Servi-Car. As the forty five was updated, so was the Servi-Car. Final drive was via a modified, fully enclosed automobile differential.**

LEFT **The Hydra Glide front end was fitted to the Servi-Car in 1958. Solid steel rear wheels had first appeared in 1951.**

RIGHT **Many police departments used the Servi-Car for dispensing parking tickets. Pre the meter, one method was to cruise around and chalk the tires of parked cars. If the car was still there past the alloted time when the officer returned from his "rounds," you were in trouble.**

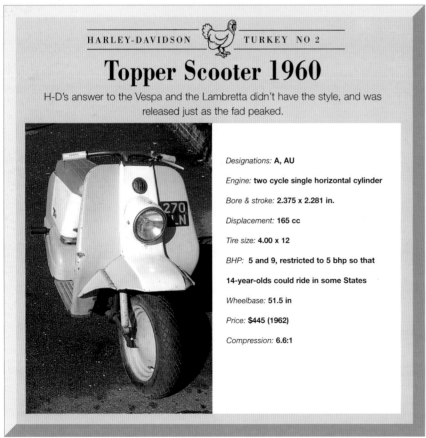

HARLEY-DAVIDSON   TURKEY NO 2

Topper Scooter 1960

H-D's answer to the Vespa and the Lambretta didn't have the style, and was released just as the fad peaked.

Designations: **A, AU**

Engine: **two cycle single horizontal cylinder**

Bore & stroke: **2.375 x 2.281 in.**

Displacement: **165 cc**

Tire size: **4.00 x 12**

BHP: **5 and 9, restricted to 5 bhp so that 14-year-olds could ride in some States**

Wheelbase: **51.5 in**

Price: **$445 (1962)**

Compression: **6.6:1**

THE ITALIAN CONNECTION

H-D had been producing its own single cylinder two strokes, the 125 cc Hummer (1947-53) upgraded to the 165 cc Super Ten and a trail version, the Ranger. From 1961 it would also produce the 175 cc Pacer, Scat and Bobcat. But the most important lightweights would come from Italy's Aermacchi. H-D needed to improve their two strokes, based upon the pre-war DKW RT125, and in particular they needed a good 250 cc machine. Aermacchi's Ala Verde fitted the bill, and was sold in the US as the Sprint. Very soon, 75% of the Varese factory's machines were being exported to the US, and the Sprint was on sale in roadster, road racer and motocrosser guise. Having sold the 250 problem – or at least put up some kind of a fight against the products from Norton, Moto Guzzi et al.– H-D released in 1964 the M50 moped and M50 S lightweight motorcycle. As H-D engines are prone to do, the 50 ccs grew to 63.86 cc in the following year. With the 125 cc Rapido in 1967 and the 100 cc Baja (1971), the latter designed for desert racing, the company had a good range of motorcycles being produced at a fast rate and selling well.

But not everything was rosy. In 1974, Varese built a record 45,000 machines. This rapid expansion involved the use of unskilled, inexperienced labor, and a consequent drop in quality. Words like "shabby" and "cheap" were used in the press about the SX 125. a lot of warranty claims were processed by a lot of disgruntled dealers.

H-D made a big effort to improve matters in the mid-1970s – now of course with AMF money to invest. Things did get better, with changes like heavier duty chains on the 125s, better air filters, better chrome finish. But AMF pulled the plug on the Varese connection just as things were beginning to come together nicely, in May 1978.

So did that mean disaster for the Italian factory? Hardly. Today it's known as Cagiva, the most successful European motorcycle manufacturer around.

The Castiglioni brothers bought the Aermacchi name and by 1982 had also acquired that of Ducati. Today, the company controls Husqvarna, Moto Morini, MV Agusta and CZ. Its competition success is outstanding and its small capacity two strokes and sport models are state-of-the-art.

HOME-GROWN BABIES

While this book was being designed, a commercial artist and motorcycle fanatic (though not an H-D rider) looked over the author's shoulder and pointed to a picture of an Aermacchi Sprint: "That's not a Harley." Then pointing to the picture of the 1957 Model 165: "Ah, now that is."

It is an interesting distinction, and one that is quite odd; following the 1969 takeover by AMF, all models, whether Italian-built or home grown, carried the same AMF-Harley-Davidson logo, though motorcycles sold in Europe were labelled Aermacchi until 1972. Nevertheless, to keep the critic happy, we should look more closely at the

"genuine" US-built smaller capacity machines.

The 125 cc machine offered in 1947 was quite a departure for H-D, based as mentioned earlier on the DKW RT125, as was the successful BSA Bantam, more or less an example of war reparations. "More or less," because both Moto Morini in Italy and Yamaha would also produce copies postwar!

Like all the others, H-D's 125 was of unit construction with a three-speed gearbox. The aluminum alloy cylinder had a 14 mm sparking plug and compression was 6.5:1. Kick start and gear levers were on the near side. The girder forks of the 3 hp machine became telescopic in 1951, and the M125 became the Teleglide. The 125 capacity machine disappeared for a year (1954), in favor of

BELOW **The 125 cc single cylinder engine, with 6.6:1 compression ratio, 2.0635 x 2.281 in bore and stroke. Kick start and foot shift.**

the 9 hp 165cc, then was reintroduced alongside the larger engine until 1959.

Though the 165cc machine, known as the Hummer, could provide 9 hp, in the US, where fourteen-year-olds could ride them, the output was restricted to 5 hp on the BTU model. "Here it is … The new Hummer! Famous Harley-Davidson quality at a new, low price!" That was the point of course: you could buy a little of the reflected glory of the big V-twins by riding a baby brother.

In the years from 1947 to 1960, more than 100,000 customers had bought into the idea. The emphasis was on cheap fun, exemplified by the names of the three lightweights introduced in 1962.

The Pacer, Scat and Ranger were all designed for a different purpose, but all were single cylinder two-strokes. The 165 cc Ranger was an off-road version of the Super-Ten, with 18-in wheeels and no lights. There was no rear suspension, and the machine was gone by 1963, when the other two gained it. The rear springs under the engine was a crude but quite effective system. The 175 cc Pacer was a conventional road machine, with a low level exhaust sys-

tem. In between the two was the Scat, a trailie before the term was invented, supposed to be adapted to both road and rough. a few year later, in 1965, the 175 ccs got a facelift in the guise of the Bobcat. While retaining the Scat frame and suspension, a number of fiberglas components were added to the model, such as the seat base and the tank. The effect was quite slabsided and the seat base looked very awkward, not to say uncomfortable.

"TOPS UNDER THE CHRISTMAS TREE"

1960 saw the arrival of the Topper H scooter. The horizontally mounted single cylinder was the old 165 cc engine. The scooter was an automatic. "These are fun wheels the whole family can enjoy with super gas mileage economy to boot! The Topper H is easy to ride, with SCOOTAWAY automatic transmission – just turn the throttle and away you go!"

Perhaps David K Wright's analysis is the most succinct in *The Harley-Davidson Official Ninety-Year History*:

"How many Harley-Davidsons can you name that had a parking brake? Or a starting system that involved neither kicking nor any kind of electrics? Or a buddy seat wherein there was room for a six pack? Or belt drive? Sound like your kind of bike? Sorry to report that was no one's kind of bike, but rather was the 165 cc Topper scooter."

3,801 Model A scooters were built in 1960, just 976 in 1963, 500 AHs in 1965, and that was it. Apart from the fact that the Topper didn't have the looks of the Italian imports, the craze never took off in the US with anything like the same enthusiasm as it did in Europe.

One other of the Milwaukee Minnows deserves attention. The Baja/SR 100 (1970-74) was a very effective offroad machine, but it soon fell behind the Japanese technologically.

The Baja gained a class win in the Greenhorn Enduro, got lights in 1972 and an automatic gas-oil feed the following year, but Honda and Yamaha has won the hearts of the young offroaders. as they had with other smaller capacity machinery.

Though the success of Harley-Davidson in competition on the smaller machines, discussed in the next chapter, is another aspect of the baby brothers which demands respect.

HARLEY-DAVIDSON   TURKEY NO 3

SX250 & SX125 1974

The SX250 never seriously challenged the Japanese trail bikes; "The motorcyclist'
in August that year called the SX125 "shabby" and "cheap."

It is of course unfair to label these machines as complete turkeys; they were actually
pretty trouble-free. What let them down was build quality. 1974 was the record year
for production out of Varese, and H-D simply couldn't hold the whole thing together.

The highlights then, (and some of the lowlights)
of the small capacity Harley-Davidson machines:

1926-1934   The side valve and then ohv single,
the Peashooter

1929-1934   The Model C, 30.5 cu in, known
as the "Baby Harley."

1929-1952   The bomb-proof Flathead Forty
Five; ftom 1932-74, as the Servi-Car.

1947-1953   The 125 cc Hummer, which
grew into:

1953-1962   The 165 cc Teleglide, Super Ten
and Ranger.

1960-1965   The Topper Scooter.

1961-1966   The US-built 175 cc Pacer, Scat
and Bobcat, and from Italy, probably the
most important in terms of the bottom line:

1961-1969   the 250 cc Sprint.

OPPOSITE, BELOW
The Italian SX250 trail bike, 1976. Come on, is that such a bad looking machine?

LEFT Or this? It is unfair that the AMF era is oftern associated with the smaller capacity machines and their various problems. AMF made the Evo revolution possible after all … and in fact, the objections to the baby brothers are not always logical. To some, it feels like an insult to the marque for it to have *ever* lent its name to anything smaller than a Sixty One!

LEFT To be honest, the names AMF and Harley-Davidson wouldn't spring to mind unless they were on the fairing! The aristocrats Bimota provided a frame for an Aermacchi/H-D 500 cc GP racer, pictured here at Le Mans in 1975. Michel Rougerie was seventh. It was a remarkable and often forgotten effort by H-D to become a force in the blue riband 500 cc Championship. Without the success of Walter Villa this experiment wouldn't have happened; and without Aermacchi's Sprint, Villa's victories would have belonged to another marque.

In 1969 the Sprint became the SS (road) 350 and in 1972 the SX (on/offroad) also got the larger engine. Aermacchi also produced machines such as the failed MX250 Motocrosser (1977); and the engine for the Shortster. There were several little machines produced during the AMF era: most of them, to be honest, were forgettable. But in competition, the Sprint had one spectacular outcome …

Low On The Hog

From board Track to Superbike

"We laid our plans for a racer ... to carry the name of the marque and the country successfully to every corner of the world."

JOE CRAIG, RACER AND DESIGNER, NORTON, 1929

Walter Davidson's win in the 1908 Long Island Endurance Run - against 22 other motorcycle makes - was great publicity, but racing soon left the standard production machines behind, and required special equipment. Was it therefore such a good idea to spend money on racing, particularly as amateurs who did well could be used in advertising without expense and without putting the company's reputation on the line?

In 1914, however, H-D decided to enter the racing arena, and the works team – the Wrecking Crew, as they came to be known – appeared for the first time in the 1914 Dodge City 300-mile race. No laurels, but from then on, with eight-valve twins and four-valve singles which were far superior in performance to the standard road machines, the Harley-Davidson works team began to dominate. Multiple entries, through which Harley-Davidson could increase their chances of victory, became a feature. Banked board racing was frighteningly fast, and the machines, without brakes, were lapping at over a ton at the beginning of the 1920s. The ohv single, the Peashooter, wasn't available to the pub-

lic, nor the multiple-valve twins. Racing was a professional closed shop dominated by Works teams, and had alienated itself from the everyday rider. In 1934, the American Motorcycling Association, (established in 1923) introduced Group C racing. This was for standard production machines, of which at least 25 had to have been offered for sale to the public. Harley-Davidson and Indian controlled the AMA by this time, and it comes as no

surprise that the Classic C rules specified the use of 45 cu in side-valves and 30.5 cu in singles, because that's what they both were making. Class C was a logical extension of the thinking behind the 350cc "Peashooter" racing that had been introduced in 1925. The larger twins could be entered for TT with its twists and jumps. Alongside Class C, open capacity Class A full professional - i.e. Works team - racing continued, and Class B semi-professional events. Throughout the 1910s and 1920s Harley-Davidson competed successfully in England, which helped exports considerably.

The star of the tracks and hill climbs of the late 1920s and 1930s was undoubtedly Joe Petrali. Apart from a brief flirtation with Excelsior, Joe, who had begun racing on Indian singles, was the jewel in the H-D racing crown for more than a decade. In 1935 he won all 13 AMA National Championship 350cc dirt track races. In 1937 he took one of the new 61 ohv twins to Daytona with streamlining and set a new record of 136.183 mph.

The 61EL Knucklehead owed much to his own experiments with carburation. For good measure, he took a 45 cu in up and down the sand for a new record of 102.04 mph. He was hillclimb National Champion for five seasons straight, 1932-1936. One of his greatest achievements was probably sur-

viving his racing career; while the efforts to reduce speed, particularly on the board tracks, had helped to lessen the mortality rate, racing was still a perilous game. Leslie "Rod" Parkhurst, a stalwart of the prewar and postwar Works team took a spill in 1915 at Rockford, Illinois, which was supposed to have, quite literally, dislodged his brain! It didn't warn him off though, and he returned to campaign a 61 cu in machine, establishing new speed records at Daytona in 1920. Most of Joe Petrali's success was garnered without factory backing; in the 1930s, hardly surprisingly, both Indian and H-D had pressing business to attend to, and factory support had more or less vanished by the late 1930s.

Though in 1937 H-D produced the WLDR 45 with aluminium heads, (and the same designation again in 1940) but for a hotter machine designed for racing. In 1941, the company produced the WR, a true racer. There was a racing department under Harvey (Hank) Syvertson, who had prepared the machinery for Joe Petrali's record attempts, but it didn't run a team, it prepared machinery and sold it, or sometimes loaned it, to deserving causes. The Indian Scout had been running away from the W series, and the company didn't approve.

By this time, board racing had faded to be replaced by flat, or dirt, track. Two versions of the racing model were produced, the WR for flat track, and the WRTT. Still, side-valves like the WL production machine but with magneto ignition,

improved valve configuration and cams, larger ports, with a strengthened lighter frame were provided for the WR.

How did they do? Well, the history of Daytona Beach as the classic road race, (albeit half on sand) begins in 1937, and a glance at the results tells the story. A battle with Indian, the British spoiling the party, then disaster in 1952, but a win out of nowhere in 1953.

It wasn't really out of nowhere of course. For some time the WR 45s hadn't been quick enough to catch the Nortons and Triumphs. The Featherbed Manx Norton, with its double loop main members, was a brilliantly simple base for racing success. The "Garden Gate" frame and the double ohc engine was too reliable and too fast. Similarly, the Indian Scout 45 cu in 648 racers had been ahead of the game. The turning point had come in 1952 with the Harley-Davidson Model K, a machine which represented the most extensive redesign ever carried out by the company on the trusty V-twin. Although it was still a 750cc side-valve, as in the W series, a lot of it was new, unit construction of engine, gearbox

and clutch assemblies. There was a foot change, a double loop cradle frame, swinging arm rear suspension and telescopic front forks. In addition to the basic roadster line, the new Ks were also offered as the KRTT road racer/TT model and the KR rigid-framed flat tracker. Technically, the racing KRTT/KR engines differed from their roadster brothers in detail rather than basics. The high point

of the 1953 Harley-Davidson racing effort came at the Daytona 200, with Paul Goldsmith's victory, at a new race record average of 94.45 mph - made all the sweeter following several years of British victories. The 1954 Daytona 200-miler witnessed a reversal in fortunes for the Milwaukee V-twins, with BSA scooping the first five places, a feat not repeated until the rise of Yamaha some two decades later. However, the rest of the AMA's racing season was dominated by Joe Leonard riding a Harley KR. Leonard won eight out of a total of 18 events in the 1954 championship, including the Laconia '100'.

Tom Sifton, formerly a San José motorcycle dealer, was the man who tuned Leonard's engine. Sifton's engineering skill gave Leonard an engine which offered around 50 bhp at the rear wheel - outstanding for a 750 side-valver in the early 1950s. His main efforts to improve power output had gone into porting the cylinders, improving cam profiles

ABOVE **The two WR racers in the foreground in this Dutch motorcycle museum have Triumph gearboxes and Hunt magnetos.**

RIGHT **One of these people is perhaps the greatest Harley-Davidson racer of the modern era. Another could be Barbara Bush (unconfirmed). Cal Rayborn (left), Daytona 1969.**

and fitting dual coil valve springs, the latter from the noted Triumph expert, Tom Witham. Other improvements concerned sodium-filled valves, chrome-plated stainless piston rings and the use of larger big-end rollers. At the end of the 1954 season Tom Sifton was persuaded to part with his super special KR Leonard motor, in fact he sold the complete machine to his friend and Harley-Davidson dealer, Leonard Andres. Andres' son Brad was then about to start his first season in the AMA expert ratings. The Sifton-tuned ex-Leonard machine proved its worth by assisting the 19-year-old Andres Junior to win the 1955 Daytona 200-miler at a record average speed of 94.57 mph. Brad Andres went on to win several other events on the AMA championship trail, including the Laconia '100', Dodge City '75' and the Langhorne '100'.

He emerged at the season's close as the AMA No.1 plate holder - the only 'rookie' ever to have done so; Everett Brasher was second, with Joe Leonard third. All three were Harley-Davidson mounted; in fact only two events in the 17-round season went to non-Harley-Davidson riders that

year. The level of success brought about a change in the rule book in November 1955; at their annual conference AMA officials voted to allow the maximum allowable compression ratio for the following season to be raised from 8:1 to 9:1, a decision which only helped Harley's British rivals. It should be noted that the KRs were then running a compression ratio in the region of 6.5:1. Nevertheless in 1956 H-D machinery took all seven title rounds. Although Joe Leonard won only two, the Mile at San Mateo, California and the TT at Peoria, Illinois, he still amassed enough points to reclaim the AMA No.1 from Brad Andres who finished second in the championship race. In 1957, Leonard not only won the championship, but half of the eight races, including his first Daytona 200 victory. For a change his nearest challenger was not another Harley man, but Al Gunter. Gunter, who was later to win fame on four wheels, rode a 499cc Gold Star; another Beeza rider, Dick Klamfoth was third. Most noteworthy was the emergence of Carroll Resweber who finished fourth, his points tally including two national victories: the half-miles at

ABOVE **No, this isn't racing, but where would you feature this remarkable achievement? Across the bizarre desert of the Bonneville Salt Flats, in 1970 Cal Rayborn took the world motorcycle speed record for the flying mile, at an average of 255.37 mph. The V-twin engine was increased to 1480 cc – and pump gas was used! The next day he averaged 260+ one way, but the engine blew on the way back. Imagine that moment if you dare, when you have worked out the not- quite-ideal vision from inside a two-foot-high orange cigar tube.**

Columbus, Ohio, and St. Paul, Minnesota. The year 1957 also saw veteran Harley-Davidson race chief Hank Syvertson retire, to be replaced by Dick (OB) O'Brien.

The following year, 1958, Carroll Resweber was champion, a position he was to hold for a record-breaking four seasons in a row, all on Harley-Davidson machinery. As for the foreign invaders, BSA was the main challenge to Harley-Davidson supremacy, with its Gold Star single and ohv twins scoring several individual national victories.

During Resweber's reign (1958-1961) Harley's other leading riders (besides Joe Leonard) were Brad Andres, Everett Brasher, Duane Buchanan, Troy Lee, Bart Markel and Roger Reiman. The last two individuals were both destined to become future AMA champions.

April 1960 brought news of the link-up between the Italian Aermacchi company and the Milwaukee factory. This gave Harley-Davidson the chance to market (and race) Aermacchi machinery in the US; with spectacular results.

The 1962 season got underway with Don Burnett winning the coveted Daytons 200-miler on a 500 Triumph twin, ending a string of seven consecutive Harley victories in this famous event. The year's AMA champion was 27-year-old Bart Markel from Flint, Michigan. Bart took over from Carroll Resweber when the four-time champ was involved in an horrific accident at the Lincoln, Illinois five-mile championship race in September. At that time Resweber led Markel 44 points to 40 and it had appeared that Resweber was heading for his fifth consecutive No.1 plate. But this was not to be. Jack Goulsen, Dick Klamfoth and Resweber all went down heavily during a practice lap.

Goulson was killed instantly, Resweber injured a leg so badly that he was destined never to race again and Klamfoth was so sickened after the experience that he hung up his leathers there and then. Markel went on to take the title with 58 points, Resweber's tally staying on 44; then came Dick Mann riding a combination of BSA (Gold Star) and Matchless (G50) machinery. Dick Mann was champion in 1963 - but only after a lot of bitter controversy concerning his Matchless G50. Mann took the title by a single point from H-D's teamsters George Roeder and Ralph White. The rising popularity of small capacity bikes led to a 250 cc AMA National Championship. The 1963 event was staged at the Peoria, Illinois TT circuit. Bart Markel won, riding a Harley (read Aermacchi) ohv Sprint. *Cycle World* tested both the Sprint and the latest KR (actually the Jerry Branch-tuned machines raced by Dick Hammer). The Sprint achieved 116 mph, the KR 142 mph. Prices for the standard over-the-counter racers were $900 and $1,295 respectively, and power output figures were quoted for the Sprint at 28.5 bhp 9500 rpm; KR 48 bhp 6800rpm. The Grand Prix effort began in 1960 with entries of the ohv flat single "Ala Verde" – remember, for production machines, Ala Verde = 250 Sprint in the US, ridden by Alberto Pagani. Fifth at Spa Francorchamps in Belgium that year, behind three MV Agustas and Mike Hailwood (fourth) on a Ducati twin. Not impressed? Everyone was at the

ABOVE **In the 1970s, there was another "Wrecking Crew" with the likes of Rayborn, Reiman and Lawwill to the fore. But they could never quite gain the total domination of their forerunners, even on home ground, despite the best efforts of the company to influence the AMA in favor of the XR750.**

LEFT **Mert Lawwill in 1970. He had actually been won over to the Milwaukee marque way back in the early 1950s.**

ABOVE **Roger Reiman, (here at Daytona in 1971), another of the excellent H-D racers of modern times. Exactly a decade earlier, he had won the Daytona 200 on a KR750.**

RIGHT **The engine of the 250 cc two-stroke from Varese, which would be developed and win the World Championship with Walter Villa three years in a row, 1974-76.**

time: the Ardennes course is notoriously fast and the new kid on the block had really surprised the established works teams. Bore and stroke were changed for 1962 and power upped to 28 bhp at 9500 rpm, plus a much-needed five-speed gearbox. You could buy one and race it yourself in 1961 if you had the money - and could find a machine. The company underestimated demand, always a gratifying and agonizing experience. Factory-supported riders competed in Europe only in GP for 1964, and won incredible fourth places in the German and Italian GPs. The engine grew to 380 or 402 cc for

European racing before the end of the decade, but the introduction of the Yamaha and TR-2 twins sounded the GP death knell for the single cylinder Aermacchi machine in 1969.

Five years later, the 250 water-cooled twin was ready for Walter Villa to take GP racing by storm. On the RR250, he won three consecutive 250 World Championships, 1974-6. In 1977, just to prove how easy it was, he took the 350 World Championship. These are the only world championships won by H-D, and as far as can be seen, they always will be.

CENTRE **In 1966, Renzo Pasolini was third in the FIM 350 cc World Championship on this kind of machine, courtesy the engineers and designers of Aermacchi.**

ABOVE **That man Cal, in the lead again, this time in the Anglo-American Series, 1972.**

Track meeting at Hinsdale, Illinois. Roger Reiman scored his second consecutive Daytona 200 victory in March 1965, but in the season-long AMA championship series it was Bart Markel who upheld Harley's honor against a flood of British bikes from BSA, Triumph and Matchless; while Dick Mann became the first rider of a Japanese machine to win an AMA National when he took his Yamaha TD-1 twin to victory in the 250 cc race at Nelson Ledges, Ohio. It was also the first time a two-stroke had won an AMA National.

Markel was again No.1 in 1966, carried to success aboard the latest version of the long-running KR side-valver. But generally the American marque had a tough year with Triumph machinery taking many of the honors, including victory at Daytona.

By the mid-1960s, racing a side valve anywhere outside the USA you would rightly have been considered hopelessly optimistic. FIM regulations classified engines by capacity and, on that basis, it was common knowledge that the side valve was much less efficient than the overhead valve or overhead camshaft designs. But American racing of the period was ruled by the AMA and not the FIM: the side

The Aermacchi competition machines were not only seen in Europe; some campaigned the RR 250 (the production version of the factory racers) in AMA events in the 1970s, and a dirt tracker was developed from the SX 250 trail bike, the MX 250. The Varese racing effort would come to an end before the MX 250 could prove itself, as the transatlantic ties were severed.

Meanwhile, in 1964 Harley-Davidson returned to the top of the AMA's championship pile, the rider this time being Roger Reiman; his two victories in the 17-round series came at Daytona and the Short

RIGHT **Canadian Davis Seal** on a works machine, Daytona 1973.

BELOW **Tim Priesler** on a 2000 cc Harley-Davidson at the Supernationals in November the same year. Drag racing is an American invention, and H-D machinery has always been the favorite choice at home. But even in this rarefied field of endeavour, the American record holder for the ¼ mile, (7.08 seconds, Bo O'Brechta) was on a Kawasaki!

valve (read Harley-Davidson!) was allowed 750 cc (more with permitted over-boring) while ohv engines were limited to 500 cc.

Another restriction which had long favored the home-grown Harleys against the foreign invaders was the ceiling on compression ratios, though this had been allowed to climb slowly from 7.5:1 to 9:1 over the previous two decades. The lower figure was just about as high a ratio as could be squeezed from a tuned side valve, with its large, sprawling valve pocket; but it blunted the edge of a British production racer just enough. Even so, getting a side-valve 750 through the speed traps at around 145 mph was still a marvelous achievement. A one-off 883 cc ohv XLR Sportster engine was fitted into a special 'Low Boy' frame and raced by the Californian Lance Weil on British short circuits during 1967. It won 1000 cc races at Lydden Hill, Brands Hatch, Oulton Park and Mallory Park, and in the process created a considerable amount of publicity on both sides of the Atlantic. After its defeats at the hands of Triumph during 1967, Harley-Davidson made an amazing come-back to the AMA racing scene with a revitalized KR model for 1968-9. Much of 1967 had been spent on development work by Dick O'Brien and his team of engineers. At the center of this was a 'Low Boy' chassis of the type first used on Weil's machine and special accessories such as gas tank, seat and, most important of all, a wind tunnel-tested fairing: these latter components were the work of the Wixom Bros. of Long Beach, California. Although Dick O'Brien never revealed the exact power output figures for the revised 1968 works KR, they were over 60 bhp at the rear wheel with the rpm now up to over 7000. Harley-Davidson gained some 8 mph on lap speeds at Daytona, with Roger Reiman setting the fastest qualifying speed for the 1968 200-miler at 149.080 mph. In the race Cal Rayborn went on to lap all but second and third by the end of 40 laps; he also became the first rider to win the event at an average speed of over 100 mph.

Only eight KR 750s were built in 1969 – all team bikes. They all employed Italian Ceriani front

XR750 Racer 1970

Dominant on the dirt ovals, as here with Scott Parker, the XR750 also acquitted itself well on the road

Designations: **XR**
Engine: **ohv V-twin**
Bore & stroke: **3.125 x 2.983 in.**
Displacement: **45 cu. in.**
Suspension: **Telescopic forks, rear swing arm**
BHP: **62 (untuned)**
Top speed: **145 mph (Daytona 1970)**
Dry weight: **320 lbs**

forks and massive Fontana four leading shoe front drum brakes, with an American-made single hydraulically-operated disc at the rear. Cal Rayborn again dominated the proceedings at Daytona and team mate Mert Lawwill took the championship.

But 1969 was also to see the end of the KR era (the AMA were introducing a new more open 750

ABOVE **In the pits with the H-D team at Daytona 200, 1971, over-heating a constant problem. Victory for Dick Mann at the Speedway that year on a BSA, before the Japanese onslaught.**

91

category for 1970) and the company taken over by AMF. The Harley-Davidson race shop, headed by Dick O'Brien, was faced with some real headaches, brought about by the new set of AMA rules and the fact that AMF, focused on production figures, didn't see racing as a priority. Even so, O'Brien tried. The result was first displayed to the public at the Houston Show, Texas in February 1970; the XR 750, designed by Dutchman Pieter Zylstra.

The prototype was built within a four month period. Although supposedly a new design, it owed much to the old KR side valve (cycle parts) and the standard production XL Sportster (engine). Lined up against machines such as the BSA/Triumph triples, the Honda CB 750 four and Ducati V-twin, the 'new' Harley was obviously going to find life difficult, at least on the tarmac.

The Daytona race exemplified the 1970 season; unmitigated disaster. Officially H-D blamed piston failures, but the troubles were not that simple and far more widespread. Most of these problems centered around too much heat. The "iron" XR 750 motor soon gained a salutory nickname, the "Waffle Iron", and this was to be the prime cause of the team machines' breakdowns during the championship season with awful regularity. Of the 25 races counting towards the AMA title, Harley-Davidson only won seven – defending champion Mert Lawwill eventually finished sixth, the best of the Milwaukee teamsters. This was also the company's lowest-ever finish in the national championship.

During the closed season break, O'Brien and his men carried out a mini-redesign and reworked cylinder heads, new crank fly-wheels (forged steel and with the mainshaft also forged as an integral part of the flywheel); the heads were now held in place with long through studs into the crankcases instead of separate bolts from case to barrel and from barrel to head.

In road racing events Cal Rayborn showed himself to be a true master of the craft, at least while his bike kept going. Even though he was down on speed he rode like no one else in Stateside road racing during 1970 and 1971, but the machine just

wouldn't see it through. The old "Waffle Iron" did have one weekend of glory, when Rayborn amazed the British by winning three of the six Anglo-American Match Races over Easter 1972 on an iron XR 750 prepared by Walt Faulk. The British team included the likes of multi-world champion Phil Read, Peter Williams, John Cooper and Ray Pickrell.

Harley-Davidson decided something must be done to salvage their tarnished racing reputation. That something was the new alloy-engined XR 750, which appeared in time for the 1972 AMA championship season. Unfortunately for Cal Rayborn and H-D, the large capacity Japanese two-strokes, not to mention the new wave European 750 four-strokes, were by this time also on the American scene. There were now Yamaha, Suzuki and Kawasaki two-strokes in addition to the four-strokes, such as the BSA/Triumph triples.

The first the world saw (and it was only a glimpse) of the prototype alloy-engined XR was at Ontario in October 1971. Then it was tucked away inside the big Harley-Davidson race transporter. Harley's Dick O'Brien told members of the press

FAR LEFT **Team Obsolete rider Dave Roper on the way to victory in the very first Battle of the Twins at Daytona in 1982.**

LEFT **Walter Villa wins the 250 cc World Championship for the first time.**

LEFT **One of Walter Villa's victories that year was at the Dutch TT. That's Kenny Roberts on a Yamaha behind, making his European GP debut.**

that the team intended to stay at Ontario after the meeting so that Rayborn and Brelsford could make tests. Following Rayborn's superb showing in the 1971 Easter Match Races, he returned to England that September for the Race of the Year at Mallory Park. This time he had one of the latest model alloy-engined XR 750s and full factory support (something he didn't have for his original visit). In the race he duelled with Yamaha works GP star, Jarno Saarinen, until the Harley's magneto expired.

After the lean years of 1970 and 1971, 1972 was a relief, with Mark Brelsford becoming the new AMA national champion. The Harley rider scored a total of 1483 points; the nearest challenger was Triumph-mounted Gary Scott on 1105. Other leading contenders that year included Gene Romero (Triumph), Kenny Roberts (Yamaha), Chuck Almgren (Yamaha), Dick Mann (BSA), Jim Rice (BSA) plus the Harley trio of Mert Lawwill, Cal Rayborn and Dave Sehl.

The following year was to prove a poor season for the Milwaukee marque. Even on the dirt, the combination of Kenny Roberts and Yamaha XS 650 vertical twin proved a serious threat to H-D's for-

mer invincibility in this particular branch of the sport. Typical of the 1973 season for Harley was the Daytona 200. Brelsford qualified at 97.954 mph (Rayborn's qualifying speed was 98.503 mph) and suffered a truly horrendous accident on lap 11 of the race, in which his machine became a fireball and he sustained two broken legs, a broken hand and a badly damaged kneecap, which sidelined the 1972 AMA Grand Champion for the rest of the year.

Later in the race Rayborn's engine seized, throwing him off the bike. In the incident he landed heavily, breaking his collarbone and suffering damaged ribs. Cal came back too soon, his collarbone not fully mended, and another incident aggravated matters. He still went to England as captain of the US squad in the annual Anglo-American Match Race Series.

In road racing for 1973, the faster and lighter two-stroke competition was much more competitive. Even Rayborn's undoubted skill couldn't make the difference. Rayborn was so frustrated by this state of affairs that he quit Harley-Davidson at the end of that year. Tragically, the 33-year-old Californian was killed whilst on his first outing on a 500 cc Suzuki twin, crashing at the Auckland, New Zealand circuit on 1 January, 1974. The Suzuki had been loaned to Rayborn so that he could compete in an international series in New Zealand. Many informed observers consider Cal Rayborn to have been America's finest road racer of the pre-Grand Prix era.

Following Rayborn's departure and subsequent fatal accident, the Milwaukee factory never repeated its road successes and (except for Battle of the Twins racing) never gained another Daytona victory with the V-twin. Harley-Davidson still produced its share of AMA champions once Kenny Roberts had departed to Europe during the late 1970s and into the 1980s, but these victories were thanks to performances on the dirt. This is where we came in. Remember that in the immediate postwar period five types of 'racing' made up the AMA Championship. One was America's own stone-age version of road racing -- in which the combatants campaigned standard issue dirt track irons and even dragged their feet through the turns. The other four, which were to remain a vital facet of Stateside competition, were half-mile, mile, short track and, most exciting of all, the TT steeplechase. The latter (no relation to the Isle of Man TT) comprised both right and left turns plus a mighty jump in which riders shot 30 or 40 feet at crowd-pleasing speed.

For short track events, engine sizes varied through the years before finally settling on a standard 250 cc maximum. Other types of dirt track racing were open to two classes, originally 45 and 80 cubic inch. But before long, rules for the national series were standardized and the maximum engine capacity was set at 750 cc. As with speedway, the machine had no brakes (rear brakes were allowed from 1970). As a result the racing was quite unique and, with speeds of over 120 mph on the longer tracks, exciting in the extreme; imagine a massive Harley V-twin drifting sideways and broadside at three figure speeds, full lock slides being needed to scrub off speed in lieu of brakes. With the advent of the 1970s the new ohv XR 750 made its debut on dirt as well as tarmac, together with a

fresh set of challengers from Japan and Europe. In the big class the XR 750 soon became a much more successful bike on the dirt than it was ever to become on the tarmac; first in the hands of Mark Brelsford and Gary Scott and later Jay Springsteen, Steve Eklund, Randy Goss, Ricky Graham and finally Scott Parker.

Of these, H-D dirt specialists, the greatest has to be Jay "Springer" Springsteen. Springer had that rare talent, as displayed by the likes of Leonard Resweber and Markel in earlier days, of a totally fearless ability to put his Harley-V-twin in front of the pack and stay there, come-what-may, until the chequered flag finally goes down. Thanks to men like these no other manufacturer comes anywhere near Harley-Davidson's record in AMA racing

For the eighties, the H-D action was in Battle for the Twins, as the XR 750 dirt track triumphs came to an end with the dominance of Honda (RS750) from 1984 onwards. The AMA series allowed Harley-Davidson back into the road racing scene, a series for souped-up production machinery, 1000cc limit. It was a way of shaking up the dominance of Yamaha and the two-stroke multi-valve racers from Suzuki and Kawasaki. The four-stroke twins could now show their mettle, and not surprisingly it quickly became a popular series in the States and in Britain. In 1983 Jay Springsteen (who else) won the BOT at Daytona. The basis of the machine was the XR1000. The rider Gene Church pulled off a series of victories in the Grand Prix class BOT series in the ensuing years. The 883 class allowed the little machines their moments of glory. Ducati were the serious opposition, and had won the first BOT in 1982. The World Superbike series provided another outlet for H-D to compete, without great success.

The latest move from Milwaukee was the 1994 unveiling of the VR1000 high tech racing machine, designed to compete in Grand Prix and AMA Superbike. This remarkable new machine is discussed in more detail in the final chapter. Remarkable, not because it hammered the European and Japanese opposition, but because it dared to try!

Harley Party
Rat Bikes and Full Dressers

'Beware of parts unknown ... Things can get grim in a hurry.'

H-D ADVERTISEMENT, 1988

ABOVE **John "Speed" Finlay from South Carolina, a man whose Rat bike has won many prizes, including Best in Class at the Rats Hole Show at Daytona; the Blue Riband event.**

RIGHT **It is not only in the US, of course, with direct involvement of the company, that H-D meets are held. This is the Brighton Rally on the south coast of England, in the year of the Evo, 1984.**

For those who believe truly, madly, deeply in all things Harley Davidson, Hog Heaven must be the black hills Motorcycle Classic. Sturgis, South Dakota, is where it all happens, the rally and races attracting more Harleys than any comparable event in the bikers calendar. For some, what is probably the ultimate in Harley parties claims their entire annual vacation; many will have traveled more than 1,000 miles, keeping their feet on the boards until they need gas, the rest room, refreshment or simply a break from the vibes. (A word to the wise: unless you want to be transformed in to a giant sun dried tomato, sun bloc is a must if you intend biking for any distance sans leathers and helmet.)

Of course, you don't have to ride a Harley-Davidson. Sturgis is for everyone who arrives on a motorcycle, rider or passenger. But Milwaukee-made muscle predominates. After all, Sturgis without Harley would be like New York without the Statue of Liberty. Most of the iron which streams into this small farming town in early August is post-Evo, but plenty of Shovels and Knuckleheads are also in attendance. Thousands of V-twins potato-

potato their way down Main Street. A look around for lookalikes will reveal clusters of customs including Viragos, Vulcans and (aptly named) Intruders. Cloning a Harley, even down to the chrome-zones, is something the Japanese big four do increasingly well (or just maybe increasingly). Their collective

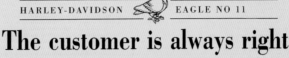

The customer is always right

Intsead of distancing itself from the parties being held by its own riders, H-D are right there these days, often with Willie G in the saddle.

This nine-wheel Harley-Davidson truck is owned and run by the factory, powered by a big twin 1340 cc engine, (naturally). When Willie G came up with the inspired FX series, he rode one at Daytona to hear the reaction firsthand.

homage to the great American machine has hugely increased the custom market and, paradoxically, actually boosted sales of the real thing.

Sturgis also welcomes classic British bikes, Bonnevilles providing enduringly popular (we're talking 650cc T120 and 750cc T140 here, not the Nippon-inspired variety). Even the odd Vincent has been known to turn up. The latest Triumph Adventurer took its bow in 1996, its 'mouth organ' tank badge and rideability enticing the more discerning customer away from the Japanese herd. The response of Harley owners to the Adventurer was warm in kissing-your-sister kind of way. Gold Wings come too, hundreds flocking to peacefully co-exist with the marque that Honda could have, just maybe, snuffed out in the 1970s. The fact that the Wing is made in the USA is symptomatic of the tremendous revival in the American motorcycle industry over the last 20 years. The Sturgis event dates back to 1938, when the town became the venue for a two-day rally and race meeting held under AMA sanction for the local Jackpine Gypsies motorcycle club. Organized by Sturgis resident and

ABOVE LEFT **The 1991 FXDB Sturgis, featuring the Dyna Glide frame, produced in celebration of the 50th anniversary of the Sturgis Rally. The FXDB Daytona – also with the long Dyna Glide look – would do the same job for 50 years of Daytona Raceweek.**

LEFT **A Rat bike at the Rat's Hole Custom Show. The owner has taken up the challenge in the correct frame of mind, and included a (dead) rat.**

Indian dealer J C 'Pappy' Hoel, some 80 members rode in from nearby Deadwood. Lead and Rapid city. Registering at rally HQ has long been part of the ritual of Sturgis. Trophies are awarded to the

ABOVE **Reminiscent of the great customiser Arlen Ness's "Two Bad," also a two-engined monster (but one which could be ridden by the skilful) this double Shovel machine is quite at home at Sturgis. The increasingly popular Bikectober Fest now gives H-D lovers two bites of the cherry at Daytona, a second one in the fall. Nitro and gas-powered action at the all-Harley Drags is the main competition draw at Sturgis, though dirt track has been part of the event from day one.**

winners in the following categories:

1. Oldest rider attending in the rally from the USA.
2. Oldest rider attending in the rally from Canada.
3. Female rider coming the longest distance from Canada.

RIGHT AND FAR RIGHT **There is eight months of work on this 1978 "Maverick." The brakes alone just stop you in your tracks …**

4. Male rider coming the longest distance from Canada.

5. Female rider coming the longest distance from the USA.

6. Male rider coming the longest distance from the USA.

7. Female rider coming the longest distance from a foreign country other than Canada.

8. Male rider coming the longest distance from a foreign country other than Canada.

After finding a parking space on Main Street – akin to squeezing a sea bass into a tin of sardines – finding a camp site could not be easier; there are literally hundreds. At bedtime, those who want to drift away to the tinkle of their V-twins had best avoid the sites inhabited by heavy metal freaks, for whom Metallica played at Concorde decibels is but a sweet lullaby. If you feel the need for secluded, quiet acres, seek the advice of your fellow campers.

RIGHT **It could almost be Daytona, but actually it's England. There's room at a Hog meet for Full Dresser Electra glides like this, alongside rat bikes and raducal chops.**

BELOW **Color-coordinated leathers are not compulsory, but can look attractive on the right person.**

CENTRE **How low can you go? Chihuahua levels reached on this extreme chop.**

If, on the other hand, you want to party on with a few cold ones, no problem. Sturgis regulars tend to go the whole nine, taking in everything the event has to offer. The Harley-Davidson Travelling show at the Rushmore Plaza center in Rapid City is a must. All of Harley's new models (including Ms Harley-Davidson) are on display, together with virtually every item in the H-D catalog, which has more accessories than Diana, Princess of Wales. The show's other attractions include HOG hospitality Room (don't forget your membership card if you want a free breakfast), the Harley-Davidson semi-trailer museum and more seminars, games and ride-outs than you can shake Willie G's beret at. The man himself is only too happy to sign autographs and indulge the faithful. The tours organised by rally HQ are an integral part of the Sturgis experience. The chance to commune with the spirit of the Old West among the Black Hills strikes a special chord inside many Harley riders.

The other great meet is at Daytona Beach, Florida in late February. Here the racing takes center stage; the classic Daytona 200 having begun in 1937, Indian winning on the 3.2-mile circuit, the Harley-Davidson VR1000 not winning in 1995! The number of riders in town is even higher than Sturgis. You should have been at the 1993 parade in Milwaukee. The traffic backed up for miles!

LEFT **Both most certainly born in the USA. Though one may be a German Shepherd, he wouldn't sit so proud on a BMW.**

BELOW **Now the XLCR was supposed to be an all-black Cafe racer with two-into-two siamesed exhaust headers. So?**

BOTTOM **The possibilities are endless at this New York dealership. "80 cu in" displayed proudly between the pots.**

Harley Today

1984-Present Day

"Do you consider your business to be as operational and profitable as it was a few years ago? If Spring 1984 isn't a banner sales event, first the dealer and then the factory will be in serious financial difficulties."

NATIONAL H-D DEALERS ALLIANCE, 1983

In 1978, AMF/Harley-Davidson went to Washington to argue a case before the International Tariff Commission. They believed that the Japanese manufacturers had been dumping over-production on the US market. The hearings were long and incredibly complex, not least because Japanese machines over 750 cc were actually manufactured in Ohio and Nebraska. The outcome, to put it as simply as possible, was that the Commission thought maybe some dumping had occurred – but that it hadn't really affected H-D's market share! This judgement must have been some kind of catalyst. The implication was that H-D needed to update its own machines, and that buying in from Aermacchi was not going to solve the problem. The Italian connection was severed, and H-D's engineers approached the AMF Chairman, Ray Tritten, to argue that an update was the only way forward.

The first outcome was an increase in capacity of the Shovelhead engine to 80 cu in on the FLH models, and then the the FX cruisers. 74 cu in disappeared with the 1979 Wide Glide. As described in chapter two, 1980 was a watershed year, with the new FLT, five-speeds and engine vibration greatly reduced in a new frame, plus the belt driven FX.

But it was all too late for AMF, they were by

then actively looking for a buyer; and they couldn't find one. At this point, perhaps, another one of the Hog's nine lives is very much under threat. Begin to count off the problems, and you can see a mountain to be climbed:

1. Your parent company wants rid of you, and everyone knows it.

2. Production from the East is ever expanding, and the machines include high tech middleweight offerings which you cannot hope to challenge either on price or on technological grounds; and even the Japanese are feeling the pinch following the OPEC oil price explosion. This means that Honda *et al* are hungry for sales and willing to keep prices down to get them.

3. Related to that explosion, interest rates are now sky high.

4. The dealership network is under immense

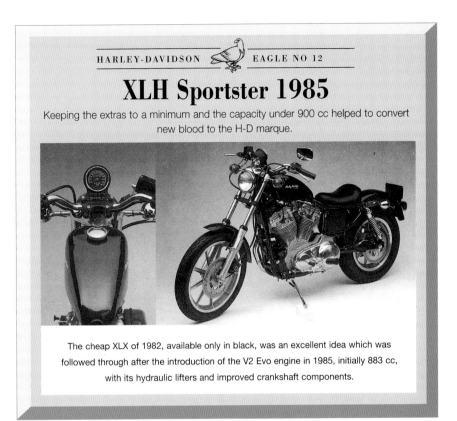

HARLEY-DAVIDSON · EAGLE NO 12

XLH Sportster 1985

Keeping the extras to a minimum and the capacity under 900 cc helped to convert new blood to the H-D marque.

The cheap XLX of 1982, available only in black, was an excellent idea which was followed through after the introduction of the V2 Evo engine in 1985, initially 883 cc, with its hydraulic lifters and improved crankshaft components.

LEFT **The FXWG Wide Glide introduced in 1980 has survived until 1997, now the FXDWG Dyna Wide Glide. The idea is still basically the same: raked out forks, and ape hanger bars.**

RIGHT **Some subtle Electra Glide candy paint phtographed at the Brighton Super Rally in England, 1984. One of the first things the new, post-AMF H-D management team tried to do was reconfirm the special relationship between company and riders all over the world, by encouraging dealers to get involved with Harley-Davidson events and establishing the Harley Owner's Group.**

CENTRE **The full Dresser Harley; today, the divide is (very roughly) between the genuine tourers like this one, the cruisers – which are in fact still low geared stump pullers – and the Sportsters.**

pressure, and there are still too many warranty claims being processed.

5. Industrial relations in the factories are not good. There had been damaging strikes in the mid 1970s.

It all looks pretty frightening, but the answer, ultimately, was pretty simple. Let the people who know what they have, who understand more intimately just what kind of magic the 45-degree, large capacity V-twin could still weave, run the company. In June 1981, a management buyout was confirmed, under the chairmanship of Vaughn L Beals Jnr, someone to whom anybody who loves Harleys owes a lot. What was one of the first things the new management did? They made a lot of noise in the trade press, in the true H-D tradtion of old. "Motorcycles by the people, for the people," appealing to that core H-D enthusiast market which had never really gone away. There was a mass ride by most of H-D's new owners from York to Milwaukee in July, to emphasise the return of the "old" H-D. another thing they did, also an echo of earlier times, was chase those trading on the H-D name without authority, the many aftermarket accessory suppliers and garages using the Harley-Davidson logo illegally.

An important change to the range itself was a new all-welded frame for the Sportster, which made it much lighter and faster. but this wasn't the majot shakeup that was surely necessary. This would come along in 1984.

EVOLUTION, NOT REVOLUTION

The retention of the "feel" of a Harley-Davidson has been essential down through the decades; whether this has been deliberate or accidental is open to debate before the last H-D engine revolution, but at that point, post-AMF, everyone involved with the company, at least within managment, knew that a revolutionary new machine was not what was required. Improvement upon what had gone before was the answer.

When, therefore, the company decided to update

its engines, partly because the riders demanded it and partly because it had to be done to meet looming 1986 Federal noise and emissions laws, it took years of patient CAD research to fettle the old Shovelhead, not some brilliant back-to-the-drawing-board breakthrough. Low maintenence was a key, and so was the look of the new block, alongside the technological refinement. With AMF's money, what emerged was a quieter, cleaner engine, with long service intervals – but as always, a V-twin with enough torque to pull an elephant's tusks.

At first glance, the V^2 Evolution engine looked like another top end revamp, like the Shovelhead and Panhead, but it was more radical. Still based upon the Shovelhead bottom end, the cylinder barrels were alloy with shrunk-in iron liners. This meant a huge improvement in hear dissipation. The combustion chamber was more effective, because the valves were less steeply inclined. The valve gear was brand new, and the old domed pistons were replaced by flat top Mahle pistons. The cylinder heads/barrels were married to the crankcase by long bolts, which "rigidified" top and bottom end. The electronic firing really was as sophisticated as anything available on a Japanese or European machine.

LEFT **FXRT Sport Glide, 1985; perhaps not as obviously different as the other FX offerings, and therefore not so successful.**

RIGHT **Heavily customised 1992 Heritage Softail.**

BELOW **Heritage Softail Custom of 1987, arguably the best year for tourer customs, before the look began, perhaps, to compromise the touring practicality of the bigger machines. The saddle bags, for example, got prettier, but smaller.**

It still vibrated of course, because it was still a 45-degree V-twin – you can't make a silk purse out of a Hog's ear – but with its new push-rod design and camshaft lift mechanism, it was more powerful, more efficient, more reliable and quieter. Praise for this feat of engineering, in the author's opinion,

cannot be too high, precisely because it was not a ground up rethink, which in so many ways is an easier task. What the H-D engineers had done was give the lie to that old saying "no sense in reinventing the wheel."

What about a nickname? Well, looking at the smooth lines of the valve covers, the best the enthusiasts could come up with was "Blockhead," which wasn't as inspired as Knucklehead, and didn't catch on so well.

The engine was actually first fitted to the FLT and FLHT models (and not all of them got it in 1984, some retaining the old Shovelhead and four speeds), but the V^2 really starred for the first time in the FXRS Sport Glide.

This machine had all the best of the new features seen across the big V-twin range in various combinations: five speeds, the isolating engine mounts, the CADCAM new frame. The advertising copy for the V^2 ran:

"A technological wonder that pumps out 10%

RIGHT **AMC Harley-Davidson special, 1994.** This one-off was built by brothers Eberhard and Richard Schwarz in Wittlingen, near Stuttgart, for customer Ernst Lauer. The Evo engine has Screamin' Eagle cams, S & S carb, and produces 70 bhp at 5000 rpm. The forks are as on the Honda Fireblade, and the frame is hand welded Reynolds 531. The exhaust is the brothers' own design.

BELOW **1990 Fat Boy;** based upon the Heritage Softail, the machine lives up to its name. Big tank, rear fender, alloy disc wheels, silver gray finish.

more horsepower, 15% more torque and with out-standing gas mileage. In five years and 750,000 miles of testing, the V^{2TM} test engines have proven low in maintenance, high in durability and absolutely tight as a drum in oil-sealing properties."

Remarkably, as this is after all an advert, it was all true! (Though you can't authenticate the miles.)

As if the introduction of the Evo wasn't enough for one year, there was another innovation, which would prove to be a stroke of marketing genius.

SOFTAIL SUCCESS

It is fairly astonishing that what the fashion writers call "TNBT," The Next Big Thing, happened to H-D thirteen years ago. Though there have been many changes in the line-up of motorcycles offered, there has been nothing quite so different as the Evo engine and the FX Softail.

The rear suspension units on this machine were cunningly hidden underneath the engine; something similar had been tried earlier on the old Scat/Pacer/Ranger lightweights way back in 1962. The suspension was hidden in this way to imitate the old hardtail look, and it worked very well. To add to the nostalgic look and feel, there was no electric start and only a four-speed 'box.

ABOVE **XL1200S, 1996,** the Sportster Sport, so good they named it twice. Effective twin discs at the front, top speed 105 mph.

CENTRE **One of the kits you can chase if you have the money. (In 1993 the company had announced that the public sale of H-D engines or transmissions as separate items for *individual* customisng efforts would be stopped.) This is the Corbin Harley-Davidson Warbird 1200. Californian seat manufacturers Corbin originally offered the fairing, spoiler, bars and seat on the FXR, now on the Sportster.**

This was no one-season styling exercise: today's line-up includes the FXSTC Softail Custom, the FXSTS Springer Softail and the FLSTC Heritage Softail Classic. And these are just the machines with the hidden monoshock rear suspension that mention the word "Softail!"

The Sportster had the V^2 engine for 1985, and there was another intelligent decision taken by Willie G and the H-D management team. The 3 x 3.8 in bore and stroke gave 883 cc's, which was ducked under the insurance band again. Partly at the urging of the dealers, who could see that there was a potentially bigger market for the Sportster outside of the short distance street cruiser ghetto it had gradually become trapped in, H-D took all the trimmings off and introduced it as an entry-level machine. At $3,995, it did indeed attract new riders to the the American Way: 10,000 in the first year. Even better, the smaller capacity Evo was not just a hacked-about version of the larger 80 cu in engine, or a reheat of the old Sportster mill.

The alloy cylinder heads, hydraulic valves lifters, flat-topped pistons and diaphragm clutch all helped to improve power and efficiency. It was so good, the company could legitimately claim that the reduction in capacity had no effect on performance in com-

parison with the old iron engine models. The motorcycle was considerably lighter at just 466 lbs. There was a very seductive buy-back option, whereby the owner could trade in his 883 Sportster after a year for any 80 cu in model, getting   full price credit against the new purchase. The Evo generation design team was led by John Favel, who came from Norton-Villiers, and the vital intricacies of gas flow were the work of Jerry Branch, founder of Flowmetrics Inc, Ca.

LIBERTY, BUELL

At the same time as this turnaround in motorcycle quality and sales, H-D had won contracts to supply shell casings to the Defense Department for the Navy. Government contracts are always good news for cash flow, because you usually get paid, (unless you pick the wrong country.)

In the same year as the stripped-down new Sportster was released, management was back in the saddle for a transcontinental ride led by Vaughn Beals and Willie G Davidson from LA to New York, as part of the celebrations following the refurbishment of the Statue of Liberty. The combination of liberty and the Great American Freedom Machine proved irresistible to the papers.

In 1986, Eric Buell, a former racer and influential H-D engineer, left the company to develop a supersports-type racing machine using a Sportster engine and gearbox. As outlined in chapter four, Harley-Davidson had faded from the competition scene in the 1980s – hardly surprisingly, considering the upheavals within the company. Buell's Battletwin employed the iron XR1000 engine, a model produced by H-D for just two years (1983-84) with twin Dell'Orto carbs and unrefined grunt. The homologated RR Battletwin, in a Bimoto-type frame, reawakened American interest in BOTT competition in 1987. Buell then produced the RS 1200 Westwind for 1990, a supersports model with Evo Sportster engine and 9:1 compression. Eric

LEFT **Eric Buell's 1996 Evo-based supersports exotic.**

ABOVE **The FXSTSB Bad Boy**, introduced in 1996. It has a slotted disc rear wheel instead of (Springer Softail) spokes, floating front disc, studded seat – and lots of black paint. Scared?

ABOVE RIGHT **1997 Heritage Springer**, with exposed springs at the front for that authentic forties/fifties look. $16,995 gets you 690 lbs of motorcycle, and 76 ft lbs @ 3500 rpm.

RIGHT **Why this machine at the end of the book? To pose the question: what is authentic Harley and what isn't … This is in fact a 1990s replica of Peter Fonda's bike in** *Easy Rider*, **a machine that was already chopped to the extreme for cinematic effect. This amazing customising feat was performed by Jim Leonard in Valencia, Ca. 1954 1200 cc engine with 1962 bottom end. A fake? No, pure Hog!**

Buell's efforts were so successful that in 1993, H-D bought 49% of the stock of the Buell Motor Company, thus giving the designer the capital to progress his development of Sportster-based high tech specials. (You can also get hold of special edition bespoke machinery today from Titan, a US company specialising in H-D jaw droppers such as the Sidewinder, 130 mph, 1573 cc, 108 bhp, price to match.)

Harley-Davidson themselves has also been busy on the competition front, announcing in 1994 the VR1000, aimed at GP and AMA Superbike. The 61-degree V-twin engine, (worked on over the pre-

vious five years) had fuel injection, liquid cooling and multi-valves. On its first outing at the Daytona 200, it stayed with the pace for 20 laps before mechanical problems. A new dual canister muffler was fitted in 1995. But troubled development since then points to one major hurdle: in order to compete with the Ducati desmo V-twin Superbike and the four-cylinder Japanese bikes, a V-twin will need positive valve operation to reach the incredibly high revs needed to be competitive.

"THE AGE-OLD URGE TO RUN AWAY"

This is the first line in the H-D 1997 catalog. It then evokes the memories of Arthur, Walter and the two Williams. Harley-Davidson is one of the few companies that can get way with this kind of refernce to past glories – that should be *allowed* to get way with it – because what H-D offers the world now is not so fifferent to what it offered nearly a century ago. H-D still even supplies machines for the US military! (Admittedly Rotax-powered.) Today, H-D could not build enough motorcycles to satisfy demand, whether with fuel injection, fitted to 80 cu in Evo models in 1995, ot without. 100,000 riders turned up at the Milwaukee 90th anniversary celebrations. The Harley Owner's Group, set up by the company in 1983, now has more members than the AMA, over a quarter of a million across the world. The 100,000 production barrier was broken for the first time in 1995.

Those marvelous engines are still built in Milwaukee!

LEFT **A perfect 1958 Duo Glide photographed at Sturgis in 1990, for comparison with the chopped Hog from tinseltown via Jim Leonard. Which one is genuine Harley-Davidson? Both are.**

OVERLEAF **a Metisse Harley-Davidson XL1000, 1995.**

As mentioned earlier, Harley-Davidson finally caught up and passed the Honda Gold Wing in domestic sales (in 1986). In the December 1996 edition of the magazine *Motorcycle International*, there was a fascinating face-off between the GL1500SE Gold Wing and FLHTCUI Ultra Classic Electra Glide. One sentence from journalist Dave Minton sums up the difficulty of defining the H-D magic: "Unlike the Wing, which revels unashamedly in self-indulgent svelt opulence, the Glide robustly boasts in every conservative form and dynamic its brawling pedigree." Two very different riding experiences from the ultimate tourers. Mr Minton also had the acuity to see that "For all its presentation, the Wing is actually built to ultra traditional standards ... by comparison with the Wing, the Glide handled like a lightweight ... Amazingly, it could be scratched with impunity." These comments are not quoted in order to defend the Glide against its great rival – it doesn't need any defending. Rather to point out that H-D riders do not remain loyal to the marque out of some kind of masochistic enjoyment of a badly set up machine. The FXSTSB Bad Boy may *look* bad, but it handles almost discreetly.

There is only enough room left now to dream a little, and consider the options from Milwaukee for 1997: 19 models, five Sportsters, seven FX hybrid cruisers, and seven FL monsters. Though admittedly the distinctions can get pretty blurred.

Sportsters: XLH 883, the smallest and cheapest, 52 bhp and 103 mph. XLH Hugger. Lower seat, more chrome, a few more dollars. XLH1200, 1200C and 1200 Sport – the Sport gets adjustable suspension at front and rear. Alloy wheels for the Sport, spokes for the Custom.

FX Series: FXD Dyna Super Glide, FXDS-CONV Dyna Convertible, FXDWG Dyna Wide Glide, FXDL Dyna Low Rider, FXSTC Softail Custom, FXSTS Springer Softail, FXSTSB Bad Boy You expect a description of that lot? Not without a bigger book. Except to say that "convertible" means an easily detachable screen, and that the Heritage Softail has a big stepped seat and a solid disc rear wheel. "Springer" of course means homage to H-D's patented Springer front forks.

FLs: FLSTF Fat Boy, FLSTC Heritage Softail Classic, FLSTS Heritage Springer, FLHT Electra Glide Standard, FLHR/RI Road King, FLHTC/CI Electra Glide Classic, FLHTCU/UI Ultra Classic Electra Glide. Confused? Probably. The Ultra Classic offers an extra two speakers, more robust leg shields, an intercom and voice-activated CB, all of which contributes to the 785 lb dry weight! No fuel injection for the Electra Glide Standard.